# The Complete Guide to Day Trading for a Living in 2019

Revealing the Best Up-to-Date Forex, Options, Stock and Swing Trading Strategies of 2019 (Beginners Guide)

*Written by Mark Vogel*

purposes only. All effort has been executed to present accurate, up to date, and reliable, complete information. No warranties of any kind are declared or implied. Readers acknowledge that the author is not engaging in the rendering of legal, financial, medical or professional advice. The content within this book has been derived from various sources. Please consult a licensed professional before attempting any techniques outlined in this book.

By reading this document, the reader agrees that under no circumstances is the author responsible for any losses, direct or indirect, which are incurred as a result of the use of information contained within this document, including, but not limited to, — errors, omissions, or inaccuracies.

# Table Of Contents

Introduction ........................................................ 16

Chapter 1 : An Introduction to Day Trading ..... 19

   About Day Trading Strategies ......................... 19

   Benefits of Day Trading .................................. 21

   General Steps to Adopt while Day Trading .... 23

   Setting up a Plan for Day Trading .................. 24
      What? .......................................................... 25
      How? ........................................................... 26
      When? ......................................................... 26
      Why? ........................................................... 27

   Importance of Strategic Planning .................. 28

Chapter 2 : Characteristics of a Day Trader ...... 32

   Knowledge is Key ............................................ 32

   Capital Requirements ..................................... 32

   Strategy ........................................................... 33

   Discipline ........................................................ 33

Chapter 3 : Day Trading for a Living ................. 35

  Day Trading Desk ............................................. 36

  News Sources .................................................... 37

  Software ............................................................ 37

Chapter 4 : 10 Basic Day Trading Tips ............. 40

  No Substitute for Knowledge ......................... 40

  Fixed Capital .................................................... 40

  Time Investment .............................................. 41

  Take Small Steps .............................................. 41

  Refrain from Penny Stocks ............................. 42

  Timing Trades .................................................. 42

  Limit Orders .................................................... 43

  Realistic with Profits ...................................... 44

  Remain Calm ................................................... 44

  Plan of Action ................................................. 44

Chapter 5 : Increasing Your Money's Worth by
Trading Options ................................................. 46

  Benefits of Using Options ............................... 50

Types of Options ........................................ 51

American options ........................................ 51

European options ........................................ 52

Short-term options ..................................... 53

Long-term options ...................................... 54

Exotic options ........................................... 55

Implementing options trade .......................... 55

Chapter 6 : Forex Trading for Beginners ........... 57

Forex as a Hedge ....................................... 57

Forex as Speculation ................................... 59

Currency as an Asset Class ........................... 61

Trading currencies ..................................... 61

Forex Trading Risks .................................... 62

Advantages and Disadvantages of Trading in Forex .................................................. 64

Forex Tips and Tricks .................................. 66

Understand your trade ................................ 66

Plan it out .............................................. 67

Broker .................................................. 67

Account type ........................................... 68

Start small ................................................68

Single currency pair ...........................69

Follow your instinct ...........................69

Losing position ......................................70

Emotions ................................................70

Journal.....................................................71

Automate trade.......................................71

Forex robots ...........................................72

Keeping it simple...................................73

Follow trends..........................................73

Forex is all about probabilities...................74

Patience ..................................................74

Follow your judgment ...........................74

Money management................................75

Technical and fundamentals...................75

Never give up...........................................76

Chapter 7 : Swing Trading Tips - Your Definitive Guide to Swing Trading ....................................77

What is 'Swing Trading' ...............................77

Day Trading vs. Swing Trading ......................78

The Commandments of Swing Trading .........80

It is important to align your trade with the direction of the market.................................82

Go long on strength and short on weakness ....................................................................83

Trade with a trend that is a time frame above the one you are trading ...............................84

Do not trade short-term chart of swing-trading time frame. ......................................85

Enter a trade closer to the beginning of a trend and not at the end.............................87

Use multiple indicators and do not trade on a single technical tool or concept...................88

Track a set group of stocks...........................90

Enter trades only if you have clear trading plans and use the four main elements of trade including limit, target, stop loss and add on point .................................................91

Try to get the odds to favor you ..................93

It will help to incorporate fundamentals and technical analysis into your trade ...............95

Swing trading can be a psychological game just as much as a game of skills ..................96

Chapter 8 : Stock Trading 101- Comprehensive
Stock Trading Tips Straight from the Experts...98

Choosing Liquid Shares....................................98

Entry and Exit Points .....................................98

Stop Loss.........................................................99

Booking Profits ...............................................99

Do not Invest ................................................100

Watchlist.......................................................100

Do Not Go Against the Market ......................101

Time the Market ...........................................101

Investment Strategies....................................101

Unfavorable Conditions................................ 102

Smaller Sum.................................................. 102

Technical Analysis ........................................ 103

Close all Positions......................................... 103

Research........................................................ 104

Trading Indicators ........................................ 104

Volatility........................................................ 104

Chapter 9 : Intraday Time Analysis ................. 106

Chapter 10 : 10-Day Trading Strategies for Starters ............................................................. 119

Look for an Imbalance in the Demand and Supply ............................................................ 123

Price Targets ................................................. 124

Have a Risk to Reward ratio in Mind ........... 124

Patience ......................................................... 125

Discipline is Key ........................................... 125

Take Action .................................................... 126

Money Worth Losing ..................................... 127

Too Much for One Trade ................................ 127

Explore the Market ....................................... 128

Second Guessing ........................................... 128

Online Help .................................................... 128

Chapter 11 : Understanding Futures/Commodity Trading .......................................................... 130

How to be Successful in Futures Trade? ...... 133

Commodities ................................................ 134

Currencies.................................................. 135

Interest Rates and Indexes ........................... 136

Getting Started............................................137

Day Trading Futures for a Living ................. 139

Who can Carry out Futures Trading?........... 140

Day Trading Futures Products for Retail Traders ...................................................141

Tips & Tricks for Day Trading Futures for a Living ......................................................141

Intuition.................................................... 142

Attitude..................................................... 142

Number of trades ...................................... 143

Fundamentals............................................ 143

Technical ................................................... 144

Bank Traders ............................................... 144

Intraday Trading Tips and Tricks ................ 145

Do's ............................................................. 147

Don'ts.......................................................... 149

Chapter 12 : Automated Training – Everything You Should Know About It .................................153

What are Automated Trading Systems?....... 154

Partner Links ...................................................155

Pros of Automated Trading Systems............ 156

Cons Associated with Automated Trading ... 160

Automated Services for Efficiency ............... 164

Chapter 13 : Trading Algorithms .......................167

Why Should You Use a Trading Algorithm? 176

Chapter 14 : The Difference Between Investing and Trading for All Traders .............................. 189

Holding Time .................................................. 193

Capital Growth................................................ 193

Risk Appetite .................................................. 194

Art vs. Skill..................................................... 194

Chapter 15 : Simple Strategies to Make Money and Profits........................................................ 196

Putting Focus on Hot Stocks ........................ 196

Short Sell ........................................................ 197

Cut Down Losses ............................................ 197

Booking Profits .............................................. 197

Keep up ........................................................... 198

Liquid Stocks ................................................. 198

Hype ................................................................. 199

Diversification and Leverage ........................ 199

Basic Strategy ................................................ 199

Make Plans ..................................................... 200

Chapter 16 : Long Term Strategies ................. 201

Ride a Winner ................................................. 201

Selling off Losers ........................................... 202

Hot Tips .......................................................... 202

Small Stuff ...................................................... 202

Short Gains ..................................................... 203

Price per Earnings Ratio ............................... 203

Penny Stocks .................................................. 203

Future Oriented ............................................. 204

Have an Open Mind.......................................204

Tax..............................................................205

Chapter 17 : Strategies for Options Traders ....206

Proper Capitalization...................................206

Risk for Appetite..........................................206

Opportunities...............................................207

Market Cycles ..............................................207

Trading Plans............................................... 208

Risk Management......................................... 208

Emotions......................................................209

Disciplined................................................... 210

Focus............................................................ 210

Commitment.................................................211

Back Testing.................................................211

Time Period ................................................. 212

Sectors......................................................... 213

Commissions ............................................... 213

Past Performances ...................................... 213

Conclusion...........................................................215

References............................................................217

# Introduction

Are you looking for a change of profession? Are you interested in taking up stock market trading for a living? Do you wish to make the most of your investments by trading in stock markets on a day-to-day basis? Well, you have come to the right place!

Stock market trading can be quite intimidating, especially if you are a beginner. There can be many aspects associated with it that you must acquaint yourself with. This book will act as your guide and introduce you to the world of stocks.

Who does not wish to make more money? Stock markets can provide you with the right avenue to make money by using the right resources. There are, however, risks to be aware of that might come your way. The main goal should be to reduce these risks and take advantage of the opportunities that the markets can provide. If you are able to hit upon the winning formula, then day trading can help you in a big way.

Success comes to those who take the right steps and can remain patient while putting in the hard work. The stock market can be highly rewarding provided you do all the right things.

This book will work as a handbook for everything related to options trading and the intent of writing it was to help others make money and a living out of investing in the stock market as I have. This book will provide you with information regarding day trading strategies and how you can come up with a plan of action to start trading immediately. Once you become aware of the different strategies, you can pick the one that will bring you maximum profits.

The information in this book is easy to understand and can help you take immediate action. Each of the chapters will cover one specific topic that will allow you to diversify your portfolio. By using the information in this book and doing some research of your own, you will be able to come up with the winning strategy. You will be prepared to take the hurdles head on and remain patient until they are cleared up.

I want to thank you for choosing this book, '*The Complete Strategy Guide to Day trading for a Living*' and hope you find this book an informative read. I hope you have a good time reading it and are upbeat about getting started on your options trading journey.

# Chapter 1 : An Introduction to Day Trading

Day trading is a stock market strategy where a trader buys and sells stocks before the market closes for the day. It is a quick trading strategy where stocks enter and exit a trader's portfolio the very same day.

## About Day Trading Strategies

Day trading is often seen as a way in which traders tend to gamble with their money as they add it in and take it out within a few hours, but this is an outdated point of view. Day traders today use strategies instead of gambling with their money. It can prove to be a diversified approach to trading stocks.

The rise of the Internet has played a big part in making day trading a viable option for people who wish to make the most of their stock investments. The Internet has proven to be a great way to buy and sell stocks from the comfort of one's home. It has pretty much replaced on the floor trading with more and more people interested in off the floor trading.

Day trading today is quite different from how it used to be once upon a time. With the evolution of trading options, several misconceptions have been put to rest. It was in the early 90's during the dotcom boom that many technology-based stocks started doing well and was followed by mass hysteria with more and more people flocking to grab their shares. It is was at this point in time that day trading gained limelight.

Before this time, stock trading was predominantly carried out by professionals, but during the advent of the Internet, anyone with a computer and an Internet connection was able to trade stocks and monitor market movement.

The trend was set and following it was the main objective for many traders who had quit their jobs to take up day trading as their main business.

Trading arcades started doing well for themselves as they gained popularity and offered the right place to traders to make maximum profits. They would share ideas and learn about the new strategies to exploit in the world of share markets. Day trading continued to grow as an investment strategy through the 2000's adding hundreds of traders a day.

Today, day trading continues to be a popular trading technique that old hands and new practice in order to draw in maximum benefits. Here are some of the benefits associated with day trading.

## Benefits of Day Trading

- Any profits or losses the trader makes can be viewed on the same day. They do not have to wait for days to know whether they have made a profit or a loss. You can check your portfolio and see where you stand.

- It is quite easy to recognize the direction

or the movement of the stocks. Traders can make informed decisions based on the direction.

- The brokerage or commission traders pay will be much less compared to regular trading.

- Day traders will be able to avoid uncertainty, as no trade will be carried forward to the next day.

- The trader is free to enter or exit the market at any time during trading hours based on his profit goals.

- There is no set limit to how much money the investor can use to engage in day trading and depends on personal preference.

- The trader is free to set daily profit targets based on the opportunities available to him.

As you can see, there are many benefits associated with day trading.

## General Steps to Adopt while Day Trading

There are a few basic steps associated with day trading that you must adopt in order to start off the right way. Some of them are discussed here.

- To begin with, read up on the topic as much as possible so that you have a fair idea of how things work in day trading. Remember that knowledge is power and the more you know the better off you will be.

- Buy a trading computer and set up according to your convenience.

- Learn about the different trading practices that exist and understand the way in which each one can pay off. Pick the one that suits your needs and convenience the best.

- Engage in understanding technical concepts such as technical analysis, fundamental analysis, financial analysis, etc.

- The next step is to start an online account with an online broker or trading platform.

- The next step is to start trading once you set up the computer and open the trading account.

## Setting up a Plan for Day Trading

When you wish to take up day trading, it is essential that you follow a plan. A day trader's plan will help you make the most of your investments. In this segment, you will discover vital information needed to come up with important trading plans regarding day trading.

You must understand that the more complex a task, the more help you need to come up with an effective plan. A strategic plan should involve all the necessary steps required to invest in the market. Here are some questions that need to be asked.

## *What?*

When it comes to addressing this part of the strategic plan, it is all about defining the type of activities that the trader would like to take up when dealing with day trading. The main idea should be to have short-term trades in mind and the risks that might be a part of the trade. The three main things to bear in mind include trend, range, and breakout. A day trader can focus on any of these three and make strategies after considering the risks involved in trade. Let us say a trader is willing to take a risk of 5% on their trading account and this comes up to about 5% for one day. As soon as the trader loses 5% of equity, then the case will be closed, and the trader will stop trading for the day. The number of chances the trader takes for the day will depend on how fast or slow he takes to reach the 5% limit.

## *How?*

The how refers to the strategy that you adopt and how you go about executing it. This can be the most important and time-consuming part of the process. It is important to go for a strategy that you think will work well for you. It does not matter how the trader sees a particular market, he must take into account the trends, range, and resistance and also pay attention to the long-term support levels. These can help the trader understand the important steps that should be taken to enter and close a profitable deal.

## *When?*

This part deals with affixing the working hours of the deal. The market will open and close at fixed hours and you must decide upon the time when you will be making the investments. Once you do your due research, you will be able to figure out the best time to invest when the market will be volatile, and you can enter and exit a stock quite easily. It is best for day traders to avoid times when the market is stable. It is generally observed that the time when a market opens is one of the most volatile times of the day. Lunch times are quite stable, as most traders will not be actively participating in trading. Closing times can be volatile before settling down for the final bell.

## Why?

This is the last bit and one of the most important aspects of strategic planning. You must figure out why you are engaging in day trading and the purpose it will serve you. You must understand what is motivating you to engage in it and whether it will pay off. There can be many reasons why traders turn to day trading and knowing some of them can help you stay on track. Some of them include being able to supplement your income, setting up a fund for retirement or education, etc. Based on your reason, you can write down your final goals so that you are able to stick with your trade. The strategy you wish to adopt will also depend on your reason, as you will know how much risk appetite you can digest.

As you know, it is not easy to trade and there are many things to bear in mind while doing so. It is essential to not feel demotivated at any time just because a particular trade has not gone your way. Expect to face highs and lows along the way and be prepared to face them in order to achieve your final goal. This will keep you motivated to stay on track and fulfill all your goals.

## Importance of Strategic Planning

It is essential to follow a strategic plan when you wish to take up day trading. The plan can help you stay on course without being distracted. Here are some aspects associated with it.

- Having a strategic plan in place can help

you identify your goals and stick with them. By defining your goals, you will be able to come up with a plan to achieve them. It will be wrong to begin investing without planning properly. Doing so will help you remain motivated and go after your goals.

- Your goals will define the type of market research that you need to perform.

- Having a strategic plan in place can help you move in the right direction and make calculated decisions that will help you achieve your goals. You will be less confused and take decisive actions.

- It will be easier to manage your emotions if you have a proper plan in place. The market can be a volatile place and you must follow a plan in order to control your emotions and avoid taking any drastic actions. It can end up being a tempting place and make you take greedy actions, but by following a plan of action, you will be able to control yourself and remain on course. A strategic plan can help to keep your emotions in check.

- A strategic plan can help you remain proactive instead of being reactive. There is a vast difference between the two. You will be able to plan for the future and be prepared to take on any situation head on. If you rely on being reactive then you will end up getting caught off-guard and not be in a position to adapt to emergency situations. If you have a strategic plan in place, then you can easily move in the chosen direction and suffer fewer losses.

- Having a strategic plan in place can give you some clarity. There will be many options in the market to go through and you can choose the one that suits your needs and convenience. If you do not have a strategic plan in place, then you will waste time thinking about which option to go with. A plan will tell you what your options are, how much you can go with, and how much you can get out of the investment.

- You will be more aware of the resources that are at your disposal.

# Chapter 2 : Characteristics of a Day Trader

It might seem like a daunting task to be a day trader, but it is not rocket science. A professional day trader will not gamble as a hobby and instead focus on maximizing his profits. These can be established traders who know exactly how a market operates. Having in-depth knowledge can help traders in a big way to know what kind of investments will help them. Here is a look at some of the aspects to understand.

## Knowledge is Key

It is essential to understand that knowledge and experience matter when it comes to day trading. It is important to understand the fundamentals if you wish to enhance your money potential.

## Capital Requirements

You will require enough capital to make the best trades. Day traders use risk capital that they are willing to lose in the market. This can prevent financial loses and also remove any emotional attachments that they might have with money that is being invested. Most day traders work with larger capitals in order to carry out effective intraday practices.

## Strategy

As discussed earlier, having a strategy is extremely important when it comes to day trading. A day trader must ask and answer questions such as why he is carrying out a particular trade, how he will be carrying it out, when to carry it out, etc. Maintaining discipline will help him produce consistent profits.

## Discipline

Having a profitable strategy in place can help you maintain discipline. Some traders, especially beginners, can end up losing money, as they will not be able to execute a deal based on their criteria. If the trader maintains discipline, then this can be avoided.

# Chapter 3 : Day Trading for a Living

When it comes to taking up day trading for a living, there are two main types to choose from, namely those who work for themselves and those who work for institutions. The former is for those who would like to work from their homes and use the limited resources available to them and the latter is for professionals who would like to associate with bigger organizations where there is more information and resources available. They might have access to a direct line, a trading desk, more capital, tips, etc. These types of traders are the ones who will look for easy profits that can be made based on the arbitrage opportunities and news events that they have direct access to.

Individual traders will have to work on their own and invest their own capital. Although they are on their own when it comes to making decisions, they will often rely on a brokerage firm for tips and guidance, but these will be limited compared to the access that traders associated with bigger firms will have. They will not take as many risks and their capital resources will be limited. They might also not be as competent as professional traders. They will prefer to deal in predictable markets where it will be easy to assess the direction in which stocks will move.

Day trading will always have more demands towards making basic financial decisions and the instruments involved. Here are some of the basic things you will need to engage in day trading.

## Day Trading Desk

One of the most important and essentials things you will need is a day trading desk. A dealing desk will provide you with information on order executions. This will be based on the price movements that will occur in the market. Say for example, if a company announces an acquisition then the trader will look at a merger arbitrage opportunity and invest early before the rest of the market starts to get in and then take advantage of the price differential.

## News Sources

The importance of news sources cannot be stressed. It is extremely important for a day trader to have access to all the important news sources. In fact, many financial experts term it as being one of the most important aspects of day trading as news sources can provide traders with vital information needed to capitalize upon the opportunities that might arise. It can pay off to tune into a finance-based channel that will have access to news articles, analytics, experts, etc.

## Software

Trading software is an important part of day trading. It can help traders interpret the trends and understand how a particular stock can move. There are more than enough analytical software to choose from and some of the key features can include the following.

<u>Automatic pattern recognition</u>: This means that traders can identify technical indicators involved such as flags and channels and also interpret complex indicators such as the Elliot wave pattern.

<u>Genetic and neural applications</u>: These are programs that make use of neural networks and genetic algorithms to come up with more accurate predictions of future price movements.

<u>Broker integration</u>: These applications are meant to integrate with the brokerage and allows for an instantaneous and automatic execution of trades. This can help to eliminate any emotions that might arise during trade and improve the execution times.

<u>Back testing</u>: This helps traders to assess strategies and how they have done in the past to predict how they will do in the future, but it is important to understand that stocks might not always follow the same patterns as they did in the past.

These tools can help traders in a big way, as they will be able to predict price momentum. If inexperienced traders engage in day trading without making use of these indicators, then they can end up losing money.

# Chapter 4 : 10 Basic Day Trading Tips

## No Substitute for Knowledge

Apart from knowledge associated with basic trading, day traders must also keep track of the latest stock market news and analysis that can affect or impact their stocks. They must be aware of breaking news and the economic outlook held by experts. These can have a big impact on a stock's price momentum. It is essential for all traders to do their homework and come up with a wish list of stocks that can be traded and keep an eye on all the news that breaks out regarding them. Traders must go through business newspapers and magazines and watch business news-based channels.

## Fixed Capital

Working with a fixed capital can help traders make confident investments. Traders who risk less than 1 to 2% of their account per trade will be able to carry out more successful trades. If the trader is working with an account consisting of $50,000 then the maximum loss per trade with a .5% risk per trade will come up to $250. Now the trader might not always lose this and will be in a good position to hold on to it based on his experience and prowess.

## Time Investment

Day trading requires a trader to put in at least four to five hours every day. It will be best not to take it up if you are unable to dedicate at least this much time. It takes time and effort to spot trends and capitalize on them. It will be important to move fast and make quick moves in order to make the most of the investment opportunities.

## Take Small Steps

When you are just starting out as a day trader, it will be best to focus on just one or two stocks and track their movement. It is easier to track limited stocks instead of focusing on too many. Smaller amounts invested in stocks will make it easier to track them and assess how your investment is doing. Buying fractions of a stock is a good idea for beginners. For example, buying just 5% of one stock and 10% of another.

## Refrain from Penny Stocks

If you are just starting out in the world of day trading, then it will be best to steer clear of penny stocks. They might look like low priced deals that can help you earn a lot, but they can be quite illiquid and change direction quite easily. If they are stocks that are less than $5, then they might end up being delisted and start being traded over the counter; so, unless you are completely sure of a penny stock and that it will pay off in a big way, it will be best to refrain from trading in them.

## Timing Trades

It will be important to time your trades. The

market is most frantic in the mornings as soon as the markets open. There will be quite a lot of volatility. If you are a seasoned trader then it will be easy to recognize the price momentum and pick the right times to make the investment, but for a beginner, it will be important to spend some time understanding how the prices move and when it will be best to enter a trade. Lunchtime hours are usually less volatile as not too many traders will be actively trading in the market. There will again be quite a bit of momentum towards closing hours.

## Limit Orders

Limit orders can serve as a great tool to minimize losses. With limit orders, you will be able to set a buying price and a selling price. This will leave you with a price guarantee. You can execute the order with greater precision and not worry about the price moving out of your set range. You are free to set the limits and can pick based on your convenience.

## Realistic with Profits

You do not have to think of making 100% profit all the time. It might be quite unrealistic to expect it. You should be satisfied with making 50 to 60% profit. Remember, the more risk appetite you have, the greater your profits can be and at the same time, your losses too; plan carefully to maximize your profits.

## Remain Calm

It is always best to remain calm and collected, especially when the market is moving unpredictably. This is a characteristic that all day traders must possess in order to make the most of their trades. Your stock decisions should be based on logic and not impulsiveness.

## Plan of Action

You must always have a plan of action ready. Successful traders will be able to move fast between plans and maintain decorum while trading. It will be best to stick with a winning formula compared to chasing profits. Most traders follow a set philosophy that states it is important to plan your trades instead of allowing emotions to guide you.

# Chapter 5 : Increasing Your Money's Worth by Trading Options

The stock market can provide traders with many options with one such option being options trading. Apart from stocks, options are traded quite often by both experienced and new hands, but options are not as popular as some of the other instruments available to traders.

Most traders look at options as a risky prospect and refrain from engaging in it, but without doing so, it will be difficult to assess whether or not they can effectively deal in options.

Options work on the basic principle of exchanging hands where the seller tries to dispose of financial instruments at a higher price, but it might not be so simple as there will be many factors to take into account such as exchange rates, volumes, etc.

An aspect of options that you should be aware of

includes derivatives. If you have dealt with the world of stocks, then you will be aware of this concept. Derivatives refer to goods that can help traders earn their incentives. In order for an option to do well, its underlying derivatives should work in its favor and should be obtained at a reasonable rate.

Options trading mainly depend on the price momentum of the derivatives and a few other conditions. It can be defined as a contract between two or more traders where one is the buyer and the other the seller.

An option is given to the buyer, which states that the financial instrument being exchanged can become valuable in the future. The seller will be paid a fee for the instrument by the buyer in order to reserve it. The seller will then keep the instrument until the buyer settles the deal by paying in full.

Options can be a great choice for those who are trying to expand their portfolio. Options can be easy to understand and adopt. Here are some things to know about options to understand the concept better.

- Any contract that will provide the buyer the right to buy a product at a certain price is called a call option

- Any agreement that will allow the buyer to sell a product at a certain price is known as a put option

- When options exchange takes place, the total sum to be paid by the buyer is called the options price

- A contract's deadline is known as the expiry date and the price is known as the strike price

These are important concepts to know if you wish to get started in the world of options trading. Apart from these, there are a few more things to know that are as follows.

- When it comes to speculation and betting, options are the best choice. The stock market can be unpredictable in nature and end up working in ways that are out of anybody's control. Often, traders can get it wrong, as they will not be able to predict price momentum correctly. In such a case, the trader can choose a call option, which will help him cash out at any point of time.

- Aside from speculation, options also allow hedging. Hedging is ideal for individual traders who will borrow a sum and invest it into options. Doing so can help them capitalize on market momentum.

- Spreading is a concept that deals with combining hedging with speculating. In case two outcomes are possible then more than one option can be played. The cost of the investment can end up being less in comparison.

- A synthetic refers to a situation where a

new contract will be created to mimic another contract without controlling it. Say a person buys and sells goods that come with the same expiry date and the price strikes thus offsetting a loss. By using synthetics, a person can increase the expiry date and hold on to the profits.

## Benefits of Using Options

Here are the benefits associated with options trading.

- Options trading can help a trader have a better understanding of the fundamentals that are involved and explore the possibilities of the options that are a part of the market.

- They can have a clear understanding of the strategies that are being used for the different options.

- Options trading can give the trader the option of being either a full-time trader or a part-time one.

- An options trader can increase profits by combining options and stocks.

- It will be easy to fix any errors and lower risk of losing out on money by engaging in options trading.

# Types of Options

There are different types of options to choose from and some of them are explained below.

### *American options*

American options are quite common. They refer to options that can help traders exercise the right of sale anytime between the purchase date and the expiry date. You are free to sell it at any time before the option expires. This is a good option to consider if you plan on investing larger sums of money in options. It makes for a good choice for those who are not confident in their trades. If you think you sold it short, then you can always repurchase it and sell it again before the next expiry date. This will help you remain invested in the option for a longer period of time. Another aspect to know about options is that you must trade it by Friday, as Friday will be the last day of the week to trade this kind of option.

### *European options*

European options are not as flexible as American options and are thus not preferred. You are only allowed to sell them at the time of expiry and not before that; so, if the price of the underlying instrument is high in between, you will still not be able to sell it. You will have to wait until it reaches the expiry date. This can cause you to lose out on quite a bit of profit. It will be a risky option to consider, especially if you are just starting out.

There is no geographic relevance when it comes to the two terms.

## *Short-term options*

Short-term options refer to those that come with shorter expiry times. This time can vary from a few weeks to a few months based on the country where they are issued. These are usually traded as intraday options. Thus, it is ideal for day trading. Beginners can use this option to learn about the concept. One disadvantage associated with this option is that the price of the underlying instrument can rise and fall without the investor being able to get back his money on his investment. If a loss arises then there might not be enough time left to recover the loss. The investor might be forced to stick with the loss. Thus, short-term options can work as good investment options as well as bad investment options. It can help you make quick money and quickly move to the next option, but you will have to be aware of the patterns and trends that will be a part of the market. You must also be able to interpret the technical tickers in order to predict the trend and maximize profits. It will be essential to control the loss and limit it to just 5%.

### *Long-term options*

Long-term options are those that are held for longer periods of time. These are not limited to just a few weeks or months and can be held for longer periods of time such as a year or more. These are good choices, as the seller will not feel pressured to sell off the options too soon. He can wait until the price is right. If the stock's high point lies after a year, then he can hold on to it until then and then sell off. If he ends up selling before that then he can buy it back and then sell it at a later point. These types of options are also known as long-term equity anticipation securities or LEAPS. These are available for many types of options such as futures and daily stocks, but some traders think this might not be a good option to consider as they will have too much time on their hands to decide whether or not to dispose of the stocks, but it will be a good option for beginners as they can observe the market and decide the best time to sell off without being rushed.

### *Exotic options*

Exotic options refer to those that are quite unique and only a few people can access. They are usually available for high-end investors. They come with greater risk and rewards. Some of these options include Asian options, barrier options, and digital options. You are free to choose one or combine the three.

## Implementing options trade

Once you become aware of the basics, you can start implementing them. Here are some tips to bear in mind.

- Let us suppose a trader has bought shares of a company that is doing well. He now must wait for the shares to go up in value before disposing of them.

- He can instead settle for options contract for the same shares. That way, he does not have to pay the full amount for the stocks or look for buyers after buying the shares.

- Suppose each of the contracts leaves the buyer with 100 shares.

- All that the trader has to do is pay a premium to the holder of the stocks to reserve it for him so that he can buy it later after paying the amount in full.

- In case the price of the stock rises then he will buy it by paying the agreed amount and not the higher amount. He can then sell it at the higher amount.

- In case the price falls, he has the option of not paying in full to buy the shares. He can forgo the shares but will lose the premium sum that was paid to reserve the stock.

# Chapter 6 : Forex Trading for Beginners

In this chapter, we will look at the basic concepts of forex trading and what it takes to become an efficient forex trader. Forex is a combination of the world's foreign exchange and refers to the exchange of foreign currencies between traders. As per the bank of international settlements, there are more than $4 trillion in forex trade.

As you know, no two currencies will carry the same value and will be based upon the country's economic standing. This difference in values gives rise to foreign exchange services and trade. Commercial and investment banks will perform speculative trades by trading one currency against another.

## Forex as a Hedge

Companies that engage in foreign exchange are at risk owing to the fluctuations that can occur, as currencies tend to go up and down in value over a course of time in their domestic markets. This usually happens when goods and services are bought from outside their domestic markets. Foreign exchange trade can help to provide a hedge currency risk by affixing a fixed rate according to which the transaction can be fulfilled.

For this to happen, the trader will buy or sell currencies in swap markets in advance, as they will lock in exchange rates. Say for example, a company sells US made products in Europe. Let us assume that one-dollar is equal to one euro at the time of manufacture. The company incurs $100 to manufacture the products and decides to sell it at 150 euros to make a profit. This means they can make a profit of $50 per unit, but in case the dollar grows stronger against the euro and is now at a rate of .80 then it will convert to $.80 to €1. This means the profit will come down to $20 per unit.

The best way to deal with this situation is if the company reduced their risk by shorting the euro and buying the dollar when they were equal in value. That way, in case the dollar rises in value then the profits would offset the lower profits from the sale of the products and in case the dollar value fell then the exchange rate would lead to greater profits from the sale of the products and end up offsetting the losses.

Engaging in this type of hedging can be done in futures markets. The trader will have an advantage as the futures contracts will be standardized and cleared by a central authority, but the currency might be less liquid compared to foreign markets that are decentralized and exist within interbank systems around the world.

## Forex as Speculation

Forex trade will be affected by many different factors such as interest rates, trade flows, tourism, etc. These can positively or negatively impact a currency's demand and supply and lead to a volatile forex market. There can always be an opportunity available to profit from forex markets. The opportunity can help to reduce one currency's value in comparison to another. Since currencies are always traded in pairs, if there is a forecast that a particular currency will weaken in value then it will indicate that another one will rise in value.

Let us look at an example; let's assume a trader expects interest rates to rise in the US compared to China when the exchange rate between the two is $.80 to one yuan. The trader will assume that the higher interest rates in the US will end up increasing the demand in the US and thus the yen to dollar exchange rate will fall as it will only need fewer stronger dollars to buy yuan.

Let us assume that the trader gets it right and the interest rate rises and the yen to dollar value drops to .50. This means a person now needs $.50 to buy one yuan. If the trader had managed to short the yuan and gone long on the dollar then he would have profited from the change in the parity of the two currencies.

## Currency as an Asset Class

When it comes to currencies being traded as an asset class, there are two main features that are as follows.

- They can help to earn an interest rate differential

- They can help to profit from changes in exchange rates

An investor can greatly profit from the difference between the two interest rates based on two different economies by buying the currency using the higher interest rate and shorting the currency using the lower interest rate.

## Trading currencies

Currency trading is now quite common. This is owing to the advent of the Internet. There was a time when traders had to undertake great difficulty to trade currencies as they did not have access to the Internet and could not get in touch with other traders. Forex trading also needed a lot of capital and, thus, it would end up being a tough trade. These days, online brokers and dealers offer high leverages to individual traders who control larger trades using a smaller account balance.

## Forex Trading Risks

Forex trade can be complicated and risky. There will be many rules and regulations to bear in mind. Forex instruments are generally not regularized or standardized. In some parts of the world, forex trade can be fully unregulated in nature.

Interbank markets can be made up of banks that trade with each other in different parts of the world. Banks will themselves need to determine and accept sovereign risks and credit risks that they have established in order to safeguard their trades. Some industry regulations can be imposed to protect the banks that are involved.

Most of the market consists of banks that provide offers and bids for specific currencies and the pricing will be based on the demand and supply. There can be larger trade that can take place within the systems; it might be a little difficult for the rogue traders to have an influence on the price momentum of the currency. The system can help to generate transparency in the market such that investors can access interbank dealings. Many of the retail traders who have smaller unregulated forex dealings can requite prices and can trade against their customers. Some dealers might have to go through government and industry regulations, but they might be inconsistent.

Many retail investors can spend time investigating a forex trade to find whether or not it is regulated in the US or UK or in countries that do not have stringent rules and regulations and oversight. It will be a good idea to find the type of account protections that are available for market crisis or in case a dealer ends up becoming insolvent.

## Advantages and Disadvantages of Trading in Forex

The advantage associated with forex is that the volume of trade can be quite high and there will be quite a bit of liquidity in the market. This will make it quite easy for traders to enter and exit trades, especially for currencies that have substantial disparity and where market conditions tend to fluctuate quite often.

Forex markets are open 24 hours a day and, thus, the trader can trade at any point of the day or night. He is free to time it with the foreign country's timings such as Sydney, Hong Kong, India, Paris, etc.

A large amount of data can be generated from the markets that can be used to predict or understand where the market is headed. It will be easier to gauge the price momentum based on such movement. The trader will also have access to the tools that are required to analyze such information.

The challenge associated with forex is that some dealers and brokers in the forex market might allow higher leverages, which means that traders tend to control bigger positions using little money at their disposal. The leverage can be quite high such as 100:1. The trader must be aware of the risks that such leverages can introduce and also the advantages associated with it. High levels of leverage can lead to dealers becoming insolvent.

Another challenge associated with currencies is that trading in them productively can require an understanding of economic fundamentals and indicators. The trader might have to have a thorough understanding of these concepts in order to be able to predict currency price movement.

The forex market is ideal for those who work with limited funds and can adopt swing trading and day trading using smaller sums. Those who have large funds and engage in long-term fundamentals-based trading can also benefit from forex. It will be key to focus on macroeconomic fundamentals that tend to drive currency values up and help forex traders become profitable.

## Forex Tips and Tricks

Forex can be a tricky trade, especially if you are just starting out. It will be important to understand the different ways in which the market can be played and how you can make the most of your investments.

### *Understand your trade*

It will be important for you to understand your needs and your particular trading style. In order to profit in the forex market, you must find markets that suit your needs. Having self-awareness can help you understand your risk tolerance and assess your capital allocation. You will have to spend time analyzing your own financial goals before engaging in forex trade.

## *Plan it out*

It is best to have a plan and stick with it. Once you determine what you are after trading, you can systematically work with a set time frame and go after your goals. Defining things such as what failure is, the time frame within which you must achieve something, what are some of the issues that might arise, etc. Answering these questions can help you have a clear vision required to remain consistent with your approach and garner bigger profits.

## *Broker*

It will be important to find the right broker especially if you are a beginner. If you end up finding an incompetent one or a fake one, then all your hard work can go down the drain. You must be able to match your trading goals with the offer made by your broker. You must understand things such as the type of client profile the broker aims to reach, the trading software being provided, the customer service and other such intricacies that might be associated with it. It will be ideal to go through reviews and testimonials before deciding on a broker.

### Account type

Once you choose the right broker, you must choose the right account type that suits your needs. It should suit your level of knowledge and expertise. As a rule, it is always best to go for brokers who charge a lower leverage. If you are good at understanding leverages, then you can opt for a standard account. If you are a novice then go through the basics of leverage and opt for a mini account to practice. The lower the risk, the better off you are as a beginner.

### Start small

One tip to follow in forex is to always start small. Use smaller sums and lower leverages in order to generate profits. There is no such rule that states larger accounts can help to generate bigger profits. If you increase your account size by using trading choices then it can be a good thing, but if not, there will be no point in adding more and more money to the account and wasting money.

## Single currency pair

It will be best to focus on a single currency pair, as it will be easier to track it compared to many currency pairs. It will be quite difficult to assess or monitor their activities. You will find it difficult to know which pair to trade. If you are working on just one pair, then it will be easier to stick with it. Choose the pair based on its liquidity.

## Follow your instinct

It is not a good idea to rely on others' advice or follow standard principles. Do what suits you the best. Do not trade based on rumors or hearsay. Do not act impulsively. You should do your own research before acting.

### *Losing position*

There is no point in adding to a losing position. You will end up losing out on money. It is impossible to say where a particular currency pair will be in the future. It will be a matter of educated guesses. If you end up adding more to a losing position, then you will end up gambling. If a trade is in the red, then it will only go back to green if the market decides so. You might not be able to influence the position by adding more money to it.

### *Emotions*

It will be important to control your emotions when trading. Excitement, greed, euphoria, and panic can all end up influencing your trade and calculations. You must control these emotions if you want your trade to go your way. The best thing is to start small or make smaller investments so that you do not get carried away.

By reducing your risk, you can remain calm and understand the long-term goals that are associated with the trade and reduce the effect of emotions on trading choices. It will be best to undertake a logical approach that is not governed by emotions.

## *Journal*

It is important to journal your journey in the market. Be it a forex market or your stock market journey in general, it is important to maintain a diary where you can write down your experiences. Mention your success stories and also your failures. Keep track of all the money that you invest. You must make sure you carefully go through all your activities so that you are aware of the steps to take in order to make better deals and follow hot trading tips.

## *Automate trade*

If you wish to make it easier for yourself and carry out trades without much effort, then consider automating your trade. If you wish to have a successful career and have a profitable run, then it will be best to automate your forex trade. It will prevent impulsive or emotion-based trading. This automation does not always need to be computerized automation. It can be your own thought processes. By taking automatic steps, you will be able to react to a situation in the desired way. That is, you don't need to improvise and can implement an automatic response to a particular situation.

### *Forex robots*

There might be many untested things out there that might give you advice on trading. It is best not to rely on them as they might end up giving you wrong information. It is always a good idea to depend on tried and tested techniques and software. It will also be a good idea to find an experienced mentor who can provide you with the best advice to deal in forex. Do not take advice from people on the Internet as they might mislead you.

## *Keeping it simple*

Keep your trade simple and easy to understand. Forex does not need to be rocket science and should not be treated as such. You don't need to be a genius to carry out profitable trades. There should be clear vision and a well-defined practice implementation that can help you achieve your goals. Do not over analyze things as you might end up making mistakes. If you have had a failure, then accept it and move on instead of delving into it too much. There is no point in rationalizing failure and it will be best to move forward.

## *Follow trends*

It might not be a good idea for a beginner to go against market trends. If you have just started out with forex then stick with pairs that the market is trading. If you decide to go against the market, then you might not be able to dispose of the pairs at the right time. Following the market can make it easier to sell the currencies.

### *Forex is all about probabilities*

Before you enter the forex market, you must understand that it operates on the principles of probability. It is about taking risks and generating greater profits. It will be important to position yourself correctly so that losses can be cut down. It will be easier to manage your risk if you position yourself based on probability.

### *Patience*

Patience is a virtue in the forex market. Do not be impatient or try to fight the market as that might not pay off. Beginners should exercise patience and wait for the right moment before engaging in trade instead of going about it impulsively.

### *Follow your judgment*

If you have an idea or opinion about a particular trade, then it might be best to implement it instead of seeking other opinions. If you do so, then you might find it tough to make a choice or come to a conclusive decision.

## Money management

Before delving into forex trading, it will be a good idea to study money management. It can help to minimize losses and maximize profits. In order to ensure that you do not gamble with your money, it will be best to implement strategies that aim to cut down losses and increase profits easily. Go through a few good books on forex trade that can leave you with ideas that can be implemented.

## Technical and fundamentals

It can always pay off well if you understand the technical and fundamentals of forex trade. It is what experienced traders use in order to undertake successful trades. If the trader gets the analysis wrong, then he can end up losing out on a good opportunity. Thus, spend some time understanding the basics and how it can be used to find trades that can be lucrative. A trader can gain an edge over others by engaging in this type of analysis. He might also take more calculated risks.

### *Never give up*

Persistence is always the key to success. You must not give up on your practice and remain persistent. It is impossible to become a millionaire overnight by trading in forex unless you are super lucky. Hard work and perseverance are the two qualities that can help you in this regard. Do not give up easily and try to remain consistent with your practice. Dedicate some time towards understanding the elements involved and the kind of trade that can pay off.

# Chapter 7 : Swing Trading Tips - Your Definitive Guide to Swing Trading

## What is 'Swing Trading'

Swing trading is a concept that tries to capture stock market gains with an overnight hold or a week's hold. Swing traders make use of technical analysis to find stocks that have a short-term price momentum. Traders can use fundamental analysis and intrinsic value of stocks apart from analyzing price trends and patterns.

Traders should act fast in order to make the most of the situations where stocks can have extraordinary potential in terms of moving upwards within a shorter time frame. This means swing trading is ideal for day traders. Large institutions that engage in trading with large stocks also adopt it. Individual traders will be able to take advantage of short-term stock movement without the need to compete with bigger traders.

Swing trading is a popular type of trade where traders will look for short-term opportunities to exploit using technical analysis. If you are interested in swing trading, then it can pay off to have knowledge about technical analysis.

Swing trading can involve holding a position that can be either long or short, overnight or over a few weeks. The main aim will be to capture a bigger price momentum compared to a regular intraday trade. Swing trading focuses on price range momentum and needs proper positioning to minimize the risk. Swing trading can include a mixture of fundamental and technical analysis. Swing trading relies on bigger time frames that can range between 15 minutes to 60 minutes to weekly charts. Swing trades can involve longer holding times in order to strike the expected price move.

## Day Trading vs. Swing Trading

If you wish to take up swing trading, then it will be important to understand the difference between swing trading and day trading. The main difference lies in the holding position time. Swing trading involves at least an overnight hold while day trading involves closing out the position before the market closes. Day trading positions are meant to be held for a single day. Swing trading can involve holding on to trade for several days to weeks. Holding it overnight can make swing traders take on risks that can be a result of ups and down in the position. By taking up swing trading, the trader will try to assume a smaller position compared to day trading and use larger positions incorporating leverages through trading margins. Swing trading can make use of overnight margins of 50% in case the account meets certain criteria such as pattern day trading by maintaining $25,000 in the equity account. Swing trading can be a little riskier if margin call triggers.

Swing traders try to find multi-day chart patterns

that might involve moving average crossovers, cup and handle patterns, head and shoulder patterns, triangles, etc. If there are reversal candlesticks such as hammers and shooting stars, then they can indicate a good trading plan. Traders might also have wider stop-losses in place while engaging in swing trading in order to match the profit target.

# The Commandments of Swing Trading

Here is looking at some of the main principles to follow when engaging in swing trading.

- It is important to align your trade with the direction of the market.

- Go long on strength and short on weakness.

- Trade with a trend that is a time frame above the one you are trading.

- Do not trade short-term chart of swing-trading time frame.

- Enter a trade closer to the beginning of a trend and not at the end.

- Use multiple indicators and do not trade on a single technical tool or concept.

- Track a set group of stocks.

- Enter trades only if you have clear trading plans and use the four main elements of trade including limit, target, stop loss and add on point.

- Try to get the odds to favor you.

- It will help to incorporate fundamentals and technical analysis into your trade.

- Swing trading can be a psychological game just as much as a game of skill.

Let us explore these aspects in detail.

### *It is important to align your trade with the direction of the market*

The best way to assess the direction of the market is by using the S&P 500. Analyzing the market's primary and intermediate trends using the S&P 500 can help you gauge the general direction in which the market is moving.

The trends can give you a clear understanding of the way in which traders can make short-term trading decisions. If they end up focusing on short-term despite trade being successful for a short time, the bigger trends can reassert themselves. Your profit potential might be limited. You will have to identify longer-term trends to ensure you go with the flow and not in the opposite direction.

It has been observed that news announcements, analyst downgrades and upgrades, earnings, hits and misses tend to occur in the direction of the larger trends. Traders should have an idea of how things stand in the S&P 500 with regard to longer periods moving averages including 40-, 30- and 10-week. It will be advisable to use charts to assess the same.

## *Go long on strength and short on weakness*

Once you become aware of the trend in the market, you must try to adopt it. Try to look for longer trades when things are bullish. Find the right short-term trades when things are bearish.

Let us take for example, it is a bearish market and the 40- and 10-week moving averages are sloping downwards and the S&P is under both. In this case, you should look for stocks to go short and not long. If possible, try to incorporate price relative with the S&P 500 into the analysis. This chart can help you find stocks that are performing well in comparison to other stocks in the market. If there is a bear market, then you should find stocks whose strength line is trending down compared to S&P. You will have to go the opposite way in the case of bull markets.

### *Trade with a trend that is a time frame above the one you are trading*

I am sure you have heard of the age-old saying that goes the trend is your friend, but the trend can keep moving and not remain a constant. Both short-term and long-term ones tend to keep switching up and, thus, it is important to stay slightly ahead of the trend.

Most short-term traders try to focus on technical analysis based on the short-term chart, but this type of analysis can end up being partial or limited as traders will not be able to see the bigger picture.

A trader should focus on all the trends and not just the primary trend while engaging in swing trading. Even if there is a bear market, there will be certain periods where intermediate trends can have a positive effect and the stock prices can go high. There can be bear market rallies that can be quite lucrative for traders. These can be fuelled by S&P 500 and other such major averages and end up moving upwards within a short period of time. Volatile stocks that have high beats can move upwards much faster.

Short-term traders too must focus on intermediate trends and how they can change and cause a counter-trend rally to take place.

***Do not trade short-term chart of swing-trading time frame.***

It will be important to analyze the trends that weekly, hourly, and daily charts might put forward. It will be important to look at both the short-term trends and the long-term trends.

It will be a good idea to look at a two-year weekly chart to find shares regarding long-term moving averages and find a consistent trend. The weekly chart can be ideal for finding the bigger picture.

The next focus should be on the 6-month daily chart. They will be able to provide details that weekly charts might not. Use short-term moving averages to find short-term trends.

Hourly charts too should be scrutinized in order to find trends that have been consistent over the last few weeks. It will be best to analyze moving averages.

The last step would be to put together all this analysis and find a trend. You will be able to assess whether the stocks are breaking out of resistance or breaking down below support lines and analyze the volume and indicators such as the RSI. You will be able to determine if you have analyzed the data correctly and whether it is going to pay off well. It can help you find a strategy to minimize risk and increase profits.

But be careful of indicators that might not be putting out the whole story. You must understand the different aspects of a particular indicator before interpreting it. For example, a symmetrical triangle can be difficult to interpret. A MACD that is giving signals one after another within a short time frame might be unreliable.

## *Enter a trade closer to the beginning of a trend and not at the end*

It is important to position yourself correctly in the market in order to make the most of your investments. Say for example a trend is moving from the 90th floor to the 70th floor, you can still enter and exit at the 80th floor in order to profit from the situation, but it will be important to enter at the right time by identifying the trend as soon as it has begun.

The faster you find the change in the trend, the lower the risk you will have to face and the bigger the profits that will come your way. It will be important to pay attention to the market averages. You must know when they have been overbought and oversold and when they might be prone to a reversal.

Some researchers rely on several types of indicators to find a trend when the whole market is prone to a reversal. Some of these indicators include the Arms index, the Volatility index, the put/call ratio etc. If the market is testing a major zone of support and resistance, then it can help you in a big way to look at highs and lows and the advance and decline lines.

A lot of the industrial and non-resource stocks can be related in terms of the direction of the overall market. If the market turns then they too can turn. There can be momentum indicators and candlesticks that can tell you exactly when a stock is likely to turn.

Trendlines and moving average crossovers can be lagging indicators that can confirm early warning signals. Based on your risk appetite, you will be able to trade either a leading or a lagging indicator. If both these types have been given out, then you can enter a trade with a higher profitability.

### *Use multiple indicators and do not trade on a single technical tool or concept*

It is important to make use of more than one indicator or chart. Your theories can be confirmed only if all the indicators point to the same thing. Say for example, candlesticks, volume, moving averages, and other indicators such as stochastic and MACD all point to the same thing then it means there is bound to be a rise or a fall in trend.

Remember that there can be no indicator that will get it right always. You must make the effort of analyzing the different aspects and find the trend that is most likely going to give you near accurate results.

Some indicators might be able to give you a clear picture in the short-term while some might in the long-term. This can vary between two to three days or months.

If you are not skilled at interpreting indicators or do not have enough knowledge regarding chart movement then you can take the help of an expert or use software that can interpret it for you. It will be important to be aware of the trends in order to make the right moves. Make sure you keep an eye on the trend that is being signaled by a majority of the indicators.

### *Track a set group of stocks*

Swing traders can sometimes get carried away and focus on too many stocks at once. It will be easier for them to move from one stock to another but doing so can lead to too many things to focus on.

It will therefore be best to focus on just one stock or a set of related stocks. That way, you do not have to worry about interpreting too many statistics and can focus on just one.

Focus on articles and news for the particular stock and observe it for at least a week or two. Go through the stock's fundamentals and any impact of the global market. This can serve as a guide to know or anticipate any trend that might occur. You must also keenly observe any stocks that might be volatile and have high liquidity.

Apart from these, you must also do your research

on the core group of stocks that are interlinked. Try to find top stocks belonging to the different sectors. Look at their charts and the trends that are standing out. Find the prices at which they make good trades. You can find stocks that are moving predictably and also those that might be undervalued.

Have reminders in place to analyze the different aspects associated with the stocks and you can be in a better position to find the ones that are going to pay off.

***Enter trades only if you have clear trading plans and use the four main elements of trade including limit, target, stop loss and add on point***

There are certain elements of trade that you must adopt if you wish to make successful trades. Right from setting a limit to a target to finding an ideal stop loss, you must hit these parameters if you wish to trade successfully.

Swing trading can sometimes lead to impulsive

buying and this might not be good for you in the long run. Although some impulsive buys can pay off, not all will be the same. You must approach trade with a clear plan and avoid gambling.

It is important to preserve your capital when trading. It is essential to make use of stop losses so that you do not end up losing too much money. If you have been observing the market, then it will be important to identify the best limits and stop orders to use in order to execute a winning trade.

In general, it will be best to limit loss to a minimum and maximize profits. It is best to set a limit based on the technical analysis. This can be a support level or a trendline. These can tell you a lot about future trends.

Using market orders that are manageable and not too large can help you move in the right direction. If you have not been observing the market, then consider entering a trade based on overnight analysis and use limit order. If there are any gaps in the market, then do not pay too much.

If you find that a stock is moving predictably, and you are able to predict the trend without an issue, then it will be best to add a little more to your position. Say you have 500 shares with you and they are doing really well. You can consider adding in about another 50 to 100 shares, but make sure you keep your eye on the stock's price as a sudden sharp decline can negatively impact your profit potential.

It can always be a good idea to find a good re-entry point after closing your deal. If you are in a good position when the stock is having an uptrend but are worried that there might be a downtrend any time, then you must assess what point can be good to re-enter.

### *Try to get the odds to favor you*

It is never a good idea to risk a dollar just to try to make a dime. You must analyze the charts and identify the risk and reward potential of a particular stock. Once you do, identify the target by carefully analyzing what the indicators point to. If you decide upon a target based on mere assumptions, then it might not work well for you.

It is advisable to get into trades that allow you to attain good profits if your calculations are correct. At the same time, the loss potential should be minimal. If possible, look for 1.6 to 1 odds.

But it might not always be possible as some market conditions might make it difficult to predict how your trade will go. Say for example, if you plan on investing in a stock that has recently seen a large move then it might mean a big decline or incline has already taken place. In such a case, a stop loss should be put into place. The profit to potential ratio will depend on how much you are willing to risk, but the risk percentage should always be lower than the profit percentage.

A swing trader will always try to read and re-read the charts until a clear pattern is established. Once it has been found, the trader will set the appropriate target. Once the trade begins, the trader again performs the analysis and might find a new target. The main aim is to cut out the losses and increase the profits. It might be fine to cut profits short if you feel like the losses are mounting.

### *It will help to incorporate fundamentals and technical analysis into your trade*

If you are a swing trader who holds positions for less than fifteen minutes, then you might not have much use for fundamentals. Swing traders, however, might require them, as they will be holding on to positions for days in a row to weeks. They can benefit quite a lot from having a better understanding of the company's fundamentals and inherent values. Aspects such as the PEG ratio can help to determine the value.

It is quite easy to understand how the two work.

You might have to spend a little time studying the two aspects of a company but it will be well worth your time and effort.

### *Swing trading can be a psychological game just as much as a game of skills*

As you know, trading involves thinking straight and putting a leash on your emotions. It will be important to hold on to a positive thought process while trading. You must not allow any bad trades to negatively impact your thought processes. It is best to learn from mistakes and move on. Think of the next trade that you will be making and start setting targets.

Many times, traders tend to beat themselves up over a bad trade and start accusing themselves. There should never be thoughts of I should have done this, or I could have done that. Implement them in your next trade.

It is not easy being a day trader and requires quite a bit of mental strength. A simple mistake can sometimes generate losses. In such a case, the trader must be able to pick himself up and move on to the next trade instead of focusing on the previous one. It is fine to be disappointed but harping over the same thing will only waste your time.

Take all your falls as learning experiences and move on strongly. Make a note of it so that it can be used in the future. It is always best to consult an expert or broker who will be able to explain to you where you went wrong and the right moves to make the next time such a thing happens.

These are the important aspects associated with swing trading. You can refer to it every once in a while, just so you equip yourself with the knowledge needed to carry out swing trading efficiently.

# Chapter 8 : Stock Trading 101- Comprehensive Stock Trading Tips Straight from the Experts

Stock trading is a good way to increase your income or take it up as your main job, but to do so, you must understand some of the main elements involved and implement strategies that can help you make the most of your investments.

Here are some tips to follow.

## Choosing Liquid Shares

Intraday trading is all about finding shares that are liquid. The more liquid they are, the faster you can dispose them off. It is advisable to find two or three large-cap shares that are highly liquid in nature. Finding mid-sized or small-cap might lead to shares that have lower trading volumes.

## Entry and Exit Points

It is key for day traders to find appropriate entry and exit points so that the target can be achieved effortlessly. Sometimes, traders will prefer to not take a risk and exit as soon as there is a slight increase in price, but this will mean taking less profit and, thus, it will be best to have an exit point in mind to exit the trade at the right time.

## Stop Loss

It will be important to set a stop loss that can automatically trigger as soon as the price of the share falls below a certain price point. This can help to limit the loss and lower chances of a bad trade. This is an important intraday aspect to implement as it can keep the trader's outlook positive.

## Booking Profits

Some intraday traders might find it tempting to continue with their trade even after reaching their target. This might not be a good thing as the price might start declining once it reaches its highest point. Thus, if you have a set target in mind, then the best thing to do is to exit at the right time instead of continuing with trade.

## Do not Invest

If you plan on being a day trader, then do not look for shares that work as investment options. The main point of becoming a day trader is to buy shares for shorter periods of time. The trader must make the investment and wait for the right time to dispose it off. It will not be advisable to hold on to such shares, as they might not grow in value.

## Watchlist

It is best to add about eight to ten shares to the watchlist and keep an eye on them. Apart from looking at their technical, go through news articles and other fundamental data that will tell you about the stock's potential. There might be news related to mergers, stock splits, dividend payout, etc. all of which might impact the stock's price.

## Do Not Go Against the Market

It is tough to predict market movement and it will be best to follow the on-going trend. Do not make the mistake of going against the market as you might end up in a vulnerable position. There might be times when there is a bull market indication but still there might be a fall in the stock's price. If you move against the market, then it will be important to exit your position in order to avoid potential losses.

## Time the Market

It will be important to time the market. The opening hours can be quite busy with a lot of volatility and prices moving up and down. It will be best to take positions between afternoon and 1pm in order to gain bigger profits.

## Investment Strategies

Whenever investors engage in day trading, it will

be important for them to have a clear understanding of how the trade works. Strategies should go beyond the basics such as finding the entry and exit. It is vital to stick with proper strategies to ensure that trade is carried out smoothly. Taking the help of a broker can help new investors master the art of becoming a great intraday investor.

## Unfavorable Conditions

If you feel like a trade is going into an unfavorable territory, then it will be best to exit it at the soonest. Do not make the mistake of remaining in the trade, as it might be difficult to find an exit point later. If conditions are not looking favorable, then exit even before the stop loss is reached as you will be able to save some of your principles.

## Smaller Sum

It is advisable to get started with intraday trading using smaller sums. Markets can be quite volatile, and it will help to decide on a sum that is not going to pinch your pocket too much. Smaller sums can give you big returns.

## Technical Analysis

It is advisable to master technical analysis before getting started with intraday trading. Right from analyzing the charts to the past performances, looking closely at a stock's activity can help you assess its future movement. Narrowing it down to just a few good stocks will help you keep an eye on them. It will be best to find liquid stocks that have a higher volume and allows traders to enter and exit their positions at the right times based on technical knowledge.

## Close all Positions

Day traders can take up several positions at once and must aim to close out all their positions before the end of the day. As soon as the target is reached, exit the position. It is also advisable to exit even if there is a loss. It will be a better choice than holding on to it.

## Research

Day trading will not be ideal for busy professionals who cannot dedicate some time to trade. Intraday trading requires at least five to six hours of time in order to monitor market movement and keep an eye on whatever is happening. It is essential to make the right call in order to ensure that you are left with greater profits.

## Trading Indicators

Following important indicators can help you enter and exit trades at the right time. There can be many different indicators such as RSI and stochastic, which will signal to you the right times to exit. Using the tools can benefit you and help to maximize your profits.

## Volatility

You must be prepared to take on volatility in the

intraday market. In fact, this market strives on volatility, as the difference in prices and the rate of fluctuations are what day traders try to capitalize upon. Some stocks might see a drastic change in price that can make you feel quite intimidated, but it will be important to find your targets and exit as soon as you hit them.

# Chapter 9 : Intraday Time Analysis

Daily charts are an important aspect of intraday trading as they represent the price movement based on daily intervals. These charts are a popular intraday trading technique and can be used to find the movement in prices that occur between the opening bell and the closing bell. There can be many ways in which these charts can be used and below are some of the ways in which intraday charts can be used to perform intraday time analysis.

Remember that day traders must know how to pick the right stocks to perform intraday trades. Often, they can end up failing at booking reasonable profits by not choosing the right stocks. Without proper knowledge, they can end up buying stocks that are not going to do well and end up suffering a loss.

- The first thing to keep in mind is that

there should always be a little room to take a loss on the investment. The loss should be at about 8% below your purchase point. This stop loss can help you safeguard your investment.

- Persistence is vital when it comes to intraday trading. Do not be discouraged if a particular trade does not go your way. You must keep at it and take notes from failure so that you do not repeat it.

- Intraday traders cannot become good at their trade overnight. It will take some time and effort from their end in order to find success.

- When starting out, it will pay to find a good brokering company that provides full service or discount brokerage services. The company will assign a good broker to you and help you find stocks that can be bought and sold the same day.

- If you are a beginner, then setting up a cash account will be advisable compared to a margin account.

- You do not need a lot of money to get started with intraday trading. As little as 500 to 1000 dollars can help you set up your intraday account.

- If you are completely new, then stick to stock trading. Starting with forex or futures might intimidate you. Going for stocks can help you learn tricks and tips and stay on course.

- Before starting out, research high-quality stocks that are doing well and can be invested in. Do not focus on any more than 20 to 30% stocks.

- Emotions should not be involved when engaging in stock market trades. Put a leash on your emotions and control your urges to buy and sell stocks impulsively. It is important to make calculated moves in the market.

- Penny stocks might not be a good choice as they can be extremely volatile. Do not buy shares whose value is less than fifteen dollars.

- Go through some of the stocks that successful day trader's deal in and how they pick these stocks. You will be able to get a clear picture of what stocks are best to engage in.

- It will be important to engage in a post analysis of the stocks that you pick out. You will be able to pick up points from both failures and success.

- If you wish to find stocks that are going to pay off in a big way, then it will be essential to engage in both fundamental and technical analysis. Fundamental analysis sees a company's earnings, growth, sales, profits, and the return on equity. It can help to reduce your choices so that you can easily pick out high-quality stocks.

- Technical analysis can involve understanding a stock's price and volume and getting the timing right based on its recent performances.

- In order to make the most of your investments, you must purchase stocks of the best companies at the right times.

- Two of the best indicators of strong stocks are higher sales and earnings.

- If you wish to buy a stock just as it comes out of its price consolidation phase, then it can help you achieve higher gains.

- Choose stocks that belong to leading sectors and industries. Going for the top gainers from these can help you reach your targets.

- Some of the best sectors to choose include technology, medical, software, entertainment, etc.

- Keep an eye on the volume of trade. It signals the number of shares that are being traded in the market.

- If you notice a sharp incline in a particular stock's price, then it indicates that there has been some favorable news about it. Remember that no stock's prices go up automatically. There will always be a driving force behind it. Knowing what the driving force is can help you buy the stocks in advance.

- Using indicators and charts can always help you stay ahead. Understanding cup and handle, candlestick patterns, etc. can help you predict future price rises in a better way.

- The right point to enter a trade is better

known as a pivot point which works as a good price point to get into a deal. Do not go after any stocks whose price has moved 5% beyond the pivot point.

- If a stock breaks out, then the volume should increase by 50% or more above the average.

- If there is a decrease in the price and the volume, then it can signal no significant changes in the sales.

- It might not always be a good idea to follow the age-old rule of buy low and sell high. The new age philosophy is, buy high sell higher.

- Going through chart prices and the amount and direction of volume can help you assess a stock's potential and when it should be sold.

- Remember that history tends to repeat itself in the stock market. Knowing how stocks have behaved in the past can give you an idea of how they might behave in the future.

- Most of the quality stocks can break out of the sound base and rise by 20% in about eight weeks or less from the pivot point. It will be important not to sell a stock that does so in four weeks or less as it might signal a great stock at hand.

- It will be best to track the general market by focusing on indices such as the S&P 500 and Dow Jones in order to assess the trend that has been established in the market.

- A bear market usually takes the market down by 20 to 25% and can be caused by negative news and events.

- Remember that it is not easy to go against market trends. It takes quite a lot of effort and hard work to Asses what stock will move in which direction. Four out of five stocks will always follow market trend. It can be very difficult to find the one stock that will move against the trend.

- After a distribution of about two to three weeks the market will begin to trend downwards.

- Bear markets can generate fear and uncertainty in the market. There can be many who will end up disposing of their stocks prematurely, but smart investors will enter trades at such times and wait for the market to turn around.

- Rallies refer to attempts made by a stock to advance after a bear market. The prices can move forward quickly and try to surpass its previous highs.

- Intraday traders might find psychological indicators such as put call ratios to be more helpful compared to technical indicators.

- Once you notice that your stocks are going upwards in a general market, you will have to pick better stocks.

- It is advisable to use charts and chart services that can help to find the right times to buy stocks.

- There can be winners in the market that come with stronger earnings and growth potential and can belong to leading industries.

- When it comes to investors, there can be two main types, namely value investors and growth stock investors. The latter try to find companies that have stronger earnings and sales growth and also come with bigger profit margins and a return on their equity of more than 17%.

- Investors who are after value stocks will try to find stocks that have low-profits to earnings ratio.

- When you start investing for the first time, stick to basic strategies that are easy to follow and do not complicate things. If you are looking for something basic, then ETFs make a good choice.

- Remember that low priced goods might not always be a good choice. They will be priced low for a reason and might not help you make the most of your investments.

- Options might seem like a tricky investment choice especially if you are a beginner. They can move unpredictably. The trader must be able to invest within the right time frame before the prices start to move up and down.

- Futures trades can be quite speculative in nature. Only traders who are confident in their ability to execute the trades efficiently should adopt these.

- If you have just started out with day trading, then it might not be a good idea to diversify too much as it might lead to confusion. It will be best to focus on just a few eggs in the basket instead of having too many and getting confused.

- If you are starting out with a limited budget of $500 to $5,000 then invest in just two or three good shares instead of going for too many.

- If you wish to add more stocks to your portfolio then pick out the bottom feeders and dispose of them before buying new ones.

- When buying stocks, ensure that you go for just half the number of stocks that you wish to buy. The rest can be bought after you notice a 3 to 5% rise in the value of the stock.

- Remember that almost all stocks will pull

back after their bull run at the market. If you were unable to dispose of the stock at its high, then it will be advisable to wait for it to have another run before selling.

- If a particular stock's earnings show a downward trend, then dispose it off.

# Chapter 10 : 10-Day Trading Strategies for Starters

If you are a beginner, then here are simple strategies to follow.

Day trading refers to short-term trading where stocks are bought and sold on the same day. It requires a trader to move fast between positions within a few hours of entering a trade. This makes it riskier and volatile compared to other forms of trading. In order to be a successful day trader, here are some things you must know.

To start with, you must know what exactly intraday trading incorporates. A day trade is a position that a trader enters and exits within the same day. This means it is only held for a short period of time. The trader will exit the position on the same day regardless of a profit or a loss.

The buying can involve either direct outright buying of the shares or borrowing the shares and then selling at a determined price point. The day trader or intraday trader will be after an advantageous position based on the volatility that can occur during the trading period and thereby reduce the risk of overnight changes that can be brought about once the market closes.

The level of risk involved in day trading will depend on what the trader is going after. For example, if he invests a lot of money and buys stocks that are moving unpredictably then he is bound to take more risks compared to a trader who invests only a small amount and picks predictable stocks. Since day traders do not hold their positions overnight, they can avoid any surprises that might occur in the market such as unfavorable economic conditions, political interventions, geographic interventions, etc.

A day trader does not have to think about the fundamentals of the stocks. He will be focused on the volatility involved and the previous price charts. Day traders aim to look for profits within smaller price movements based on the liquidity that can keep the markets moving smoothly compared to markets that can experience bigger price swings.

Remember that day trading cannot be viewed as a means to get rich quickly. You cannot expect to become a millionaire overnight. It takes a little time and effort and those who have an appetite for risk can make it big. If you get the basics right, then it will be quite easy to become a successful day trader.

Day trading has been popular since the early 90's but attracted bad reputation after a while as more and more home-based traders started getting in experimented with strategies that made the market extremely volatile. These new traders ended up assuming things for day trade that were not true such as being able to make a fortune overnight.

Day trading held on its own and began to become a lot less complicated once people started recognizing winning patterns and strategies. It became easier to understand and predict price momentum and go for stocks that were good options for day trading.

Some beginners can get slightly overwhelmed by what they tend to look at being too fast-paced as some of the strategies involved in day trading can be quite aggressive and move quite fast. In order to generate bigger profits, traders will have to stick to some of the strategies as otherwise it might not be easy to make the desired profits. There are online courses that can help traders learn about some of the key strategies that help with understanding the risks and rewards that can be involved in trade and how they can maximize the former and minimize the latter.

It can take some time and effort to learn the strategies but, once they are implemented, it can get progressively easier for the trader to assess the situation at hand and implement the right strategy.

Remember that it is important for traders to develop or come up with their unique or different trading styles. Following in the footsteps of others might not always be a good choice as what works for one might not work for another. Through the course of this chapter, you will read the different generic strategies that can be implemented when you wish to start off as a day trader. It can be important to modify some of the strategies to suit your individual needs.

Here are some expert tips on day trading.

# Look for an Imbalance in the Demand and Supply

Looking for an imbalance in the demand and supply can help you find the right entry points. Financial markets can be quite unpredictable and require you to put in some effort in order to attain maximum rewards. If the supply is at near exhaustion and there are buyers who are willing to buy even if the prices are going higher then it indicates a good entry point. If there is excess supply and no buyers, then the price will go down and might not be a good time to enter. It will be the first task of a novice trader to identify good entry points by going through some of the historical data available to him.

## Price Targets

The importance of setting appropriate price targets cannot be stressed. Beginners should be able to set the right price targets based on profit potential for particular stocks. If you plan on buying long positions, then it will help to know in advance how much should be your stop loss if the trade begins to go against you. If it does, then allow it to go to the stop loss and exit. Do not change your mind about it, as it might not work out well. When you set profit levels, go for acceptable levels and expect to exit a little earlier if you feel like the stock might not be able to live up to its expectations.

## Have a Risk to Reward ratio in Mind

The risk to reward ratio should be decided upon in advance as it can help you carry out the trades efficiently. A 3:1 ratio can pay off well. This will help you lose small and win big. You might not feel a pinch even if the trade does not go to plan. You will be able to exit it on time. A 5:1 is also a good ratio if you think you have hit upon a winning stock that is going to do well. Set the ratio based on experience and what has worked for you in the past.

## Patience

Day trading requires a great deal of patience. Day traders need to remain patient every day and not rush in and out of trades. Doing so can negatively impact their chances of making it big. It will be important to identify the opportunities and ensure that you stick with your principles. Once you have entered, patiently wait for your turn to exit. A good philosophy to follow is to plan your trades and then trade your plans.

## Discipline is Key

It is important, especially for beginners to

maintain a discipline and always stick with a trading plan to ensure that you make the most of your stock investments. You might have to take the help or guidance of a senior to remain motivated and go for favorable positions that pay off in a big way. Do not give into impulsive behavior as it can make you lose big. Stick with your principles and make the most of your knowledge and goodwill. Avoid focusing too much on just one aspect of the trade and spread out to focus on different elements involved.

## Take Action

If you are unable to push the sell button at the right time, then it might not be a good choice to continue as a day trader. It is extremely important to make decisions and execute them at the earliest. Pushing the order and sell button at the right times is the sign of a good day trader. It is also a good idea to automate your trades and forget about it. That way, you will not be tempted to remove the sell limit and continue chasing a higher profit.

## Money Worth Losing

It is advisable for day traders to invest money they are willing to lose. When you decide on the sum that you would like to invest, it will be best to go for a sum that you will be fine losing in the market. A successful trader will always take calculated risks and invest his own capital that he is willing to part with in case something goes wrong. Big money should be reserved for stocks that you will hold on to for longer periods of time and not invested in day trading.

## Too Much for One Trade

As mentioned earlier, it is advisable not to get too attached to just one trade and end up investing emotionally. Set a budget for a stock that should be no more than 2% to 10% of the sum at your disposal. Even if you feel like the stock is going to do very well, you must extend it to about 5% more and not more.

## Explore the Market

Once you have traded stocks for a reasonable period of time, it will be time to explore the other aspects of the market including futures, forex, etc. They too can provide good opportunities for day traders, but it will be important to understand how they work and how you can exploit them to your advantage.

## Second Guessing

There should be no room for second-guessing in the stock market. If you are a beginner, then do not spend too much time thinking or worrying about things that were out of your control. If you have followed the path you had set out to follow and yet things did not turn out the way you wanted them to then do not worry about it and move on to the next thing. Sometimes, even the right strategies can go wrong owing to wrong timing.

## Online Help

There might be some experts who can help you out by giving you good advice. Signing up for newsletters and magazines based on day trading can push you in the right direction but bear in mind that there can be some places where pumpers and bashers can exist.

# Chapter 11 : Understanding Futures/Commodity Trading

A futures contract refers to an agreement that will be signed between two parties with one being a buyer and the other a seller. The agreement will be to buy or sell an asset at a specific future date and at a set price. Each of the futures contract will stand for a specific amount of the commodity or security that has been agreed upon. Some of the most widely traded commodities are crude oil, corn, etc. There will be a vast difference in their pricing based on their worth.

Futures contracts can be seen in the same light as options contracts in terms of their usefulness when a trader wishes to hedge or speculate.

Futures contracts were designed to help farmers hedge against their prices of the crops between the time of planting and harvesting and delivered to the market. They as well as end users use futures to hedge against risk. Investors and traders of future commodities engage in speculations in order to profit by betting on the direction in which the asset might move.

The first futures contract that was introduced dealt with agricultural commodities such as livestock and grains before moving on to a variety of other assets including gold, oil, stocks, treasury bonds, etc. These included standardized contracts or agreements that would trade on futures exchanges around the world.

Before getting into the futures market, it will be important to understand the different aspects involved, how they work, and a general overview of the market.

Futures contracts refer to a type of forward contract that exists between a buyer and a seller of a specific asset. They try to come to an agreement to exchange goods or services for a future date at a price and quantity that is decided upon at the time of agreement. Future contracts are different from other types of contracts that are traded in the secondary market. They come with a wider range of underlying assets such as agricultural produce including wheat, corn, potatoes, cotton, coffee, currencies including dollars, euro, yuan, rupee, metals such as iron, gold, platinum, energy such as petroleum, oil, etc. Companies and businesses trying to hedge against risk can invest in these as well as individual investors who are trying to profit from a difference in their prices.

An important aspect associated with futures contracts is that they are standardized and regulated and free from any counterparty risks as there will be clearinghouses that will guarantee to traders in the futures market that their obligations will be honored. In order to begin trading in futures, investors must select an asset that they would like to trade and make a deposit. They will have to deposit the money with a broker, who will then place the order for the trader for the specified asset with the clearinghouse. A maintenance margin should be in place in order to keep the account functional. It will be a good idea to consider long positions.

For many investors interested in the futures market, there will be certain terms and trading strategies that might be beneficial if implemented, but a lot of them can be quite confusing, especially for beginners, but once these strategies are understood and implemented, it can pay off in a big way as the futures markets can be quite promising.

Here are some of the aspects of the market that you need to understand before starting your trade.

# How to be Successful in Futures Trade?

The futures markets are a place where hedgers and speculators come together in order to predict the future price of a commodity or currency or a market index. They will try to assess whether the price will rise or fall or remain the same.

Just as in the case of any market, futures trade comes with its own share of risks both for long-term and short-term trades. There can be a high level of volatility and substantial changes in the prices. These will depend on a variety of factors including political, geographic, economic, etc. Here are some types of futures that are traded in the market.

### *Commodities*

Commodities refer to physical products whose value is determined through the forces of demand and supply. This can include energy resources such as oil and gas, precious metals such as gold and silver, food produce such as wheat and corn, etc. These commodities are traded in a centralized market where investors and speculators come together in order to predict the future price of a specific commodity and whether it will rise, fall, or remain constant.

One strategy that can be used while trading commodities is by using straddles. These straddles are constructed by making use of the same number of calls and puts having the same strike price and expiry date. Calls refer to those where the speculator will assume that the price of the commodity will rise and put is where he assumes the price of the commodity will fall. The bottom line is that people will assume that the prices will fluctuate and remain volatile and move up or down.

The trader or speculator can also opt for a call option or a put option. We already looked at the meaning of options and the same applies here.

### *Currencies*

Just like commodities, currencies too can be traded in the market. Their prices too can be speculated. A common strategy implemented in the world of currency speculation is known as scalping. Scalping is a method where the trader known as the scalper will try to acquire short-term profits by capitalizing upon small changes that might occur in the value of the currencies. Just by doing this repeatedly, the profits can add up or multiply over time and give off a significant amount of profit when all the small profits are added up.

The time taken to make the profits can last from a minute to a few days. A scalper tries to close the deal at the earliest, but this strategy can be quite complex and not ideal for beginners, as it requires experience and discipline to carry out effectively.

## Interest Rates and Indexes

Timing the strategies can be quite important. This is especially true for traders who engage in trading indexes and interest rate futures. One of the most popular types of indexes is the S&P 500 futures contracts.

Futures contracts based on interest rates are also just as common and use timing-based trading techniques in order to carry out the trades for futures.

A cycle trading strategy can be implemented by going through the historical data and finding any possible up and down cycles for underlying assets. Two of the commonly used cycles for stock index trading are the 23-week cycle and the 14-day cycle. Understanding the price trends that are associated with the cycles can help to gain big rewards.

Seasonal trading refers to trading the commodities or currencies that can have a seasonal affect on the futures market. Data can suggest that there can be many such markets and sectors as also commodities trade that occur at varying levels through the year and showcase similar trends and patterns every year. Understanding the varying seasonal trend can be an effective way to earn more profits by trading futures.

## Getting Started

Getting started with futures markets can feel a little overwhelming especially if you are new to the world of day trading, but just with a little understanding of the simple ways in which futures work, you will be able to speculate the future and carry out trading practices by copying popular trading techniques implemented by experts. Once you get the hang of it, you will be able to carry out the trades by yourself by implementing your own strategies.

It will be helpful if you focus on the strategies mentioned in this book as it can increase your knowledge base and the level of risk you adopt. Once you feel like you have done well in these areas, you can expand your knowledge in other types of futures markets.

Trading in futures can be quite a good opportunity to diversify your portfolio and increase your profits, but it will be important to understand the different elements involved and implement the right strategies in order to make the most of your investments. Understanding the basics of futures trading can help you go a long way.

## Day Trading Futures for a Living

When it comes to trading futures, it will help to be in a volatile environment as it can benefit your trade. Experienced hands will know the importance of volatility and how it can be used to increase profit potential.

Remember that day trading futures might not be an easy task as it can involve getting used to quite a lot of things such as fluctuations, predictability, identifying the best offers, etc.

Apart from what's on offer in your local markets, you will also have to focus on things that are popular in international markets. Right from S&P 500 to Dow Jones to EURO/USD to GBP/USD to Nikkei and other popular exchanges around the world, there will be many things to investigate in order to catch the right signals and make the right predictions.

## Who can Carry out Futures Trading?

As you know, the stock market might not be ideal for everyone who wishes to earn a passive income. There can be many things to learn, understand, and implement in order to cash in on the futures market. To start with, you will need a big margin account with a clearing broker and a minimum of $5,000, but if you are looking for something more basic then you might find a few places that let you start with as little as $500.

Apart from the high cost of trading that you might incur when engaging in futures trading, you might also have to deal with high daily costs that can range from $50 to $100 based on the brokerage. This can include the desk fees that may or may not include the software, data, phone connections, exchanges, etc. The cost of trade can be as much as $2 to $4 per trade.

This means it will be important to plan out your budget in advance and ensure that you include enough capital to be able to carry out trade efficiently.

## Day Trading Futures Products for Retail Traders

Day trading in futures can be an excellent opportunity for retail traders to increase their profit potential. There can be many advantages such as reduced or no fixed costs such as desk costs, no minimum deposit requirements, etc. All these can prove to be quite advantageous for traders looking to increase their profit potential.

## Tips & Tricks for Day Trading Futures for a Living

When it comes to trading in futures, it will be important to follow a few basic tips and tricks that can help you make the most of your investments. Remember that it is essential to follow strategies that can help you stay on course. Some tips and tricks are as follows.

## *Intuition*

Day traders can focus on only a few commodities or currencies at a time instead of spreading their attention over too many things. They have the freedom to watch out for each and everything that is involved and understand things in depth. By doing so, they will be able to trade more freely and follow their instincts based on experiences and observance. Traders can learn from their experiences and implement strategies they think will work best for them.

## *Attitude*

When it comes to finding success in the world of futures trading, it will be important to approach it using the right attitude. Successful traders try to take responsibility for the trades that they carry out and ensure that they maintain discipline especially when large sums of money are being invested. These investors try not to overcompensate by trading riskily and follow strategies that they have etched for themselves.

They will work on the risk to reward ratio and ensure that they make all the right calculations.

## Number of trades

If you are a futures trader then you will be able to add more trades to the deal as the cost of trade can be less compared to other forms of trade, but if you are trading in spot products, spread bets, etc. then you might have to reduce the number of trades that you carry out per day. Spreads that pertain to major forex spreads should be low. It will be essential to make one or two trades per day if you wish to maintain consistency and make money effortlessly.

## Fundamentals

One aspect that successful traders require is an appreciation of fundamentals of the commodity being traded. Technical aspects are important no doubt, but it will also be important to focus on the fundamental aspects. Going through the history of the goods and the companies that deal with them can help to assess the price variations that might occur in the future of the products.

### *Technical*

It is also important to assess the technical of the commodities in question. Day traders will have to practice flexibility in order to take up trends and follow the flow of the trade. Some markets can be difficult to predict especially short-term ones. Traders must be able to move from long-term to short-term markets easily. It will be important to keep switching and not get caught up in just one place or type. Some indicators such as pivot points, moving averages, and RSI will be important to follow.

## Bank Traders

Many people assume that bank traders refer to banks that engage in speculative trading, but this is not true, as banks such as Goldman Sachs and Citigroup will only come up with markets for their clients and not directly engage in

---

directional trading. They will come up with quotes and take a few points from the spread.

For example, a customer wishes to buy Microsoft shares and calls Citigroup about it. The bank will buy the shares directly from the exchange and sell to the customer wishing to buy it. If the shares cost $100 then they will sell it for $100.20, which means they will be charging a risk fee of $.20 per share.

These bank traders will have a direct access to the banks in order to make the investments. They will make use of order flow and volume in order to lower the risk associated with the trade and taking into account anything that might go wrong with the business model. This means the banks are bound to benefit greatly from this type of trading. They will not lose out on anything and successfully maintain a win ratio.

## Intraday Trading Tips and Tricks

If you wish to take up intraday trading, then it

will be important to follow a few tips and tricks that can help you get started on the right foot. Here are some tips and tricks you need to follow.

- As you know, intraday trading refers to buying and selling stocks within the same day. The basic idea is to buy and sell stocks by looking at a good price to sell at in order to earn a profit.

- Trading can refer to planning and implementing ideologies in order to build a portfolio based on the requirements and the financial wellbeing of the company.

- A day-to-day analysis will be important for intraday trading based on the momentum in the market and it should reflect upon the strategies that the trader is implementing. It might not be wise to use the same strategies everywhere and change it up according to the situation at play. The trader must observe the trends in the market and customize the strategy accordingly.

- It will be a good idea to look for shares that are liquid if you wish to carry out intraday trading. The trader must find good positions so that he can exit quickly after hitting his target. It will be best to find large-cap shares.

- It is advisable to stick with the flow of the market instead of going against it. Doing so might make it difficult to evaluate the flow of the market.

Here are some dos and don'ts of intraday trading.

## Do's

- Trading refers to planning and implementing strategies by having a clear understanding of how the market operates and building a diverse portfolio that has different elements all laid out based on financial strength.

- Indicators play a very important role in intraday trading. The charts will follow a specific pattern that can be predictable in nature. Some of them include calculations that can be carried out based on stock market analysis, which will give you an idea of how things will move through the day. Having this information can make it easier for the trader to predict the movement of the stocks.

- Intraday trading can be a volatile affair as trading can be tricky. It will be important to manage emotions such as greed and fear as they can lead to losses. A person must exercise control over their emotions and ensure that they do not engage in trades that might not pay off well. It will need patience and timing the market well without becoming hasty and greedy.

- Intraday traders are required to carry out daily analysis in order to ensure that they are aware of market conditions at all times. It might not be right to use the same type of strategies in every situation and a little variety should be introduced from time to time. It is important to update the strategies and make sure it is easy to implement them in the market.

## Don'ts

- As you know, the media can tend to be a little too chaotic and confusing and end up putting out too many stories that can contradict each other. In this case, it will be best to subscribe to reliable portals that will put out reliable stories that can be used to assess the future of particular stocks and how they will move. Not all rumors should be believed, and it will be up to you to decide what is true and what is not.

- When it comes to intraday trading, you have to find shares that are going to do well for the day. This means, you don't need to think for the future of the particular stock. You only have to focus on the today and how it will pan out. Plan accordingly and you can have a good experience in the day trading market.

- When it comes to expecting profits, you must be realistic. If you have too many expectations such as becoming rich overnight then you might not be successful. If you gain in one place, then you might end up losing out in another.

- It will be important to be satisfied with what you earn from the market instead of going about thinking of what you could have earned. Satisfaction can be important when it comes to maintaining a healthy portfolio. If you are not satisfied, then you might be tempted to take more risks and end up taking bigger losses. The market will not work by rewarding you in ways you expect it to, but it will reward you if you have realistic expectations.

- Do not forget to make use of a stop loss. Regardless of how confident you are about a particular trade, it will be important to utilize a stop loss that can help you from falling down and taking losses. It can be beneficial to reduce the loss that might occur and stick to a 5 to 8% margin.

- Try to book your profits as soon as you reach your target and engage in automated trading. Do not look at the price once you dispose of your stocks. You might feel tempted to buy back and sell at a higher price, but the price might end up falling down.

- Setting daily targets is an important aspect to incorporate in trade. Set targets that are attainable and ensure that you do not forget to set targets based on your personal goals. It will help to follow set percentages so that you do not forget to set the targets for the day.

- Conducting proper research can be quite important as it will lead you to right pivot points. You will also be able to keep a tab on mergers and acquisitions and any other such news that can impact the price of the stocks.

- Do not be tempted to stay with the stock just because it is showing potential of moving upwards. Exit at the right time.

# Chapter 12 : Automated Training – Everything You Should Know About It

Traders and investors need to get their entry and exit points right in order to make the most of their investments. Money management can be easy if you use automated trading systems. These make use of computers to monitor and execute trades. This means you do not have to involve yourself in trade and can sit back and relax as your computer does all the trading. This is ideal for those who tend to get carried away by emotions and end up making the wrong moves. The computer will automatically make the decisions and execute the trades.

There can be many advantages associated with this type of trade, but it can also have some disadvantages. We will look at both these aspects in this chapter but first, let us look at some basic concepts associated with automated trading.

# What are Automated Trading Systems?

Automated trading systems refer to mechanical trading systems that use algorithms that automatically set off trading based on specific rules regarding the entry and exit points. The trader can decide upon these points and once the information is fed into the computer system, it will automatically start to execute the orders. Once the algorithm has been programmed, the trader does not need to be actively involved. The entry and exit philosophies can be based on basic rules and conditions such as moving average crossovers or some complex strategies that might need a better understanding of the programming languages that are specific to the particular trading platforms. It is best for qualified programmers to engage in the programming aspect. Some of these systems will require a direct access broker and a few specific rules that have to be written down using the platform's language. Some popular platforms such as

TradeStation platform make use of EasyLanguage, which is a specific programming language and NinjaTrader that makes use of NinjaScript programming language.

Some of the trading platforms can have strategy-building software that can help users make selections from a list of available indicators in order to come up with rules that can be used for automated trading. The users will be able to lay down longer trades that can be entered once in a while based on 50-day moving average crosses above 200-day moving average based on five-minute charts that pertain to specific trading instruments. Users are also allowed to add specific types of orders that will execute trades automatically using a particular platform's inputs.

## Partner Links

Some traders might choose a program that allows them to customize indicators and strategies and work closely with a specific programmer to come up with specific systems. This can usually need a little more effort than using a specific platform's wizard and can allow a much greater level of flexibility that can be a lot more rewarding.

Once the programmer lays down the rules, the computer will begin to automatically monitor the movement in the market in order to look for buying and selling opportunities that are based on strategies that are specific. These rules can be entered based on specific stop losses and targets. If the market is fast moving, then instantaneous order entries and exits can be introduced that can help to prevent losses in case the trade does not go as planned.

## Pros of Automated Trading Systems

There can be many pros associated with automated trading systems. Some of them are as follows.

- One of the most important pros associated with automated trading is that it helps to

Mark Vogel

minimize emotions. Automated trading can help to keep your emotions in check and make you stick to the plan. It will not make traders pull the trigger impulsively based on emotions. It will also keep them from overtrading and end up making hasty decisions that might not pay off.

- Back testing refers to trading based on historical data in order to find viable trading parameters. When a system is being designed or automated, the rules must be absolute and there should not be any room for interpretation which means the computer should not make guesses and has to be instructed on what to do. Traders must make precise modifications to rules and base them on historical data instead of taking risks in live trading. Back testing can help traders evaluate certain sets of data and fine-tune them to understand specific expectancies such as the average sum that a trader can win or lose per unit of risk undertaken.

- Automated trading can help to establish and maintain discipline and execute orders that are based on statistics and not emotions. They can help to take action in volatile markets. Discipline can refer to making trades at the right time instead of giving into emotions. These can lead to losses and end up demotivating the trader. It is also possible to prevent some human errors such as entering to sell 100 shares instead of buying them and so on.

- Following rules in trade is extremely important. Traders must follow certain rules to ensure that they do not end up altering expectancies. There can never be trading plans that can win 100% all the time. Losses will always be a part of the trading game. These losses can sometimes be quite traumatic and thus traders who undergo a few losses in a row might give up on trading altogether, but they will never know if the next trade they engaged in could have been a winner and helped them recover their losses. Some automated trading systems can help traders attain consistent results based on specific plans.

- An advantage associated with automated trading is that it can help the trader enter a deal faster. This might not be possible with manual as the trader might not be able to get his entry in fast enough and the price might end up moving. Making use of automatic trading software can help to enter trades faster and save the trader from potential losses. It can keep the trader from being demoralized if the price ends up moving upwards. It will also be easier to exit a trade without worrying about missing out on pivot points.

- Automated trading can help to diversify

the trading systems that allow the users to trade multiple accounts or strategies at a single point in time. It can have the potential to allow traders to spread their risk over different instruments and create hedges against losing their positions. It can be quite challenging for people to be as efficient to execute orders as fast as computers. Computers can look for opportunities much faster and move across different markets to find specific orders and monitor trades.

# Cons Associated with Automated Trading

There are some cons associated with automated trading and they are as follows.

- One of the main disadvantages associated with automated trading software is that if there are mechanical failures then the system might crash. The system associated with automated trading is quite simple and involves tasks such as setting up software, programming it, and allowing it to make automatic trades, but many things can wrong that might be out of the programmer's control. If the system is on a computer and not a server then it might end up losing connection with the market if the Internet connection is lost. There could be differences in theory-based trades that help to generate strategies for order platforms to turn into real trades. Some traders have to look for learning curves that start off as small-sized trades when the process is being defined.

- It will be important to monitor some of the trades. Although the whole concept of going for automated services revolves around doing away with the monitoring aspect, some systems might need monitoring to look for potential mechanical failures and connection issues and other problems such as losing power and computer crashing. These can be a part of system issues that have to be solved at the earliest in order to prevent losses. Either the trader himself or the programmer should inspect the systems from time to time to ensure that it is working optimally and there are no glitches.

- Another issue associated with automated services is that there can be over optimization. Trading systems might seem like a great idea that are easy to adopt and implement but in practice, there can be many issues associated with it that need to be addressed in order to make it an optimal option. Over optimization is one such issue that refers to excessive modifications made to the system that can lead to unreliable trading plans especially during live trading. It might be easy to make too many modifications to the strategies in order to attain expected results based on historical data on which the system has been tested. Traders can sometimes end up being incorrect by assuming that a trading plan should be 100% accurate and end up creating software that is based on unrealistic expectations. This can end up leading to failures in the live market.

- Traders have the option of running their trading systems using a server-based platform such as strategy runner. Although these might provide the perfect platform to come up with viable programs, some of them can charge fees for the system in order to help with the upkeep of the services, but most of them will work as good options, as they can provide the right platform to make modifications to the programs and perform efficient scans and searches.

As you can see, there can be many pros and cons associated with automated services. Although the pros might outweigh the cons, it is important to not treat automated systems as a replacement for executed trading. There will always be risk of mechanical failures and server-based problems that can lead to discrepancies. You might have to keep a constant eye on the system to make sure everything is going smoothly. You might have to make modifications from time to time to ensure that the system will give off accurate results, but if you are interested in using the systems the right way in order to increase your profits, then here is an in depth look at the systems.

## Automated Services for Efficiency

It is no secret that everybody loves automation as it can reduce manual labor. You can be freer and focus on other things by taking your eyes off of the charts. Although there have always been critics, automated services can be used to increase profits.

There is a lot of financial data available that can be exploited and fed into the systems in order to automate services. You can make use of API of application program interface to feed in the data. As you know, once the data is fed in, it can o a much better job at interpreting and implementing it compared to humans. Computers can be quite fast and do the work in a matter of seconds. This means you can save a lot of time and effort just by feeding data into the computer.

When system trading started, only a few pioneers were able to recognize its full benefits and implemented it to make the most of it. They were able to gain quite a lot from it and it wasn't long before others began to exploit it. Although the systems have become more efficient and easier to use, they still need efficient data to be fed in, in order to work optimally.

These systems will only interpret technical data and cannot be used to interpret fundamental data. It is therefore quite useful for a day trader who relies on technical data more than fundamental data.

Technical analysis is the study of charts and is used to assess the price patterns and the usage of indicators to find favorable market conditions. Indicators are nothing but mathematical functions of the price and volume of an asset. A pattern is nothing but just an arrangement of the prices spread over a specific timeframe.

Thus, technical trading strategies come down to numeric-based analysis and mathematics-based problems that computers can solve faster and more accurately compared to humans; so, all that a trader has to do is feed in the rules to follow and the computer will automatically do the rest.

# Chapter 13 : Trading Algorithms

An algorithm is a set of rules that need to be followed in order to make calculations and solve other problems using operations carried out by a computer. This function is quite similar to a technical trading strategy. Trading can be about decision-making and what steps you wish to adopt in a particular situation. It will be important to have a set of steps and options at hand that can be implemented in order to attain the right outcome.

A computer can help you know when to enter a trade and when to exit it. All you must do is feed in a set of data that will instruct the computer to do the same. It can be quite fast and accurate based on what you feed into the computer.

You will only be able to recognize such a system's benefits if you implement it. As and when you start using the systems, you will come face to face with the different ways in which an algorithm can replace human computation.

As you know, a computer will not get distracted and carry out a function smoothly. This is not the case with humans who can easily get distracted and end up making mistakes. It can be quite stressful to look at multiple monitors at the same time tracking various aspects of a stock, but if a computer is made to do it then it can be quite easy, and the end result can be more accurate.

A computer can handle multiple accounts at the same time. Although they will have their own limits, they can do a better job than humans. They will process data faster and put out better results that are more usable.

If you have used a trading account and received alerts whenever a stock reaches your target price, then you must know that an algorithm was used to send you the signal. Trading platforms make use of algorithms to alert users about stock prices. This can be an alert for both entry and exit points. Similarly, algorithms can help you find pivot points and make sure you enter and exit trades at the right times. The main aim is to get in and out at the right times to remain with a profit. The computer will help you do this.

Apart from automated trading, here are some other uses:

- High-Frequency Trading (HFT)

- Arbitrage trading

- Scalp trading

- Transaction cost reduction

High-frequency trading groups are those that execute large volumes of transactions at higher speeds and are thus known as high-frequency trades. As you know liquidity is an important aspect of the stock market that keeps the stocks moving at a faster pace. If there is no liquidity, then it will be difficult for traders to buy and sell the stocks. Many stock exchanges entice high-frequency trading groups to trade in the market in order to add liquidity to the market and make sure that the stocks move. They offer rebate trading to such groups. They offer incentives for carrying out certain trades in the market. This might not sound like a lot of money to make as the incentives will be quite small, but the traders will carry out millions of trades per day thus increasing the overall incentives earned.

It is only possible to make millions of trades by using computers and by no other means. Humans cannot possibly engage in trading millions of times per day. Thus, with the help of computers and automated trading, traders can trade in huge numbers on a daily basis and keep the market liquid.

The stock exchanges will incentivize the use of high-frequency trading and make decisions within microseconds. Such ones will be rewarded. If a human were to carry out the same, then it would take them forever to do so.

Although this seems like a perfect opportunity for people to make millions, some view it as an unethical practice that is not healthy for the rest of the market, but many who adopt the practice believe that they keep the market running and newcomers must adapt to it or exit the market. Markets can change constantly, and traders have to get adjusted to it at the earliest in order to remain in the game.

As you know, the whole world is becoming computerized and many people will start using automated trading. It will be important to keep up with them if you wish to make the most of your investments.

Some traders think computers will replace them in the future, but this cannot be true as computers cannot trade all by themselves and will always need to be programmed. They will require help from humans who will have to program them.

Arbitrage trading is another important aspect

associated with automated trading. Arbitrage trading refers to buying and selling that takes place at the same time in two different markets. This is now popular in the cryptocurrency markets where the price differences can be quite large between countries. People can visit another country's exchange and exchange their coins with that country.

People will take advantage of such a situation as long as it lasts. Some traders will try to take advantage of the situation by buying and selling many times a day, but it will be important to be fast and take swift action.

The best way to do this is by using computer programs. Arbitrage bots can be employed to do the same, but it might not be so easy to program a bot as they have become increasingly complex. With more and more people taking to it, it can be a little difficult to use the system to one's advantage. It will take some effort to come up with an efficient bot, but it will be important to get it going before a difference in price starts to creep in.

Some of the groups can adopt a strategy known as co-location. This is a situation where the trading company's algorithm will be hosted on a server in the same building as the exchange server so that it can be directly connected using fiber optics.

If many trading companies begin doing this then the data center will make way for fair conditions to be provided for all the groups by making use of the same length of fiber cables to connect each of the trading groups that are involved. It goes down to the same level of details that are required by all the groups involved.

Scalping is a technique that is predominantly used in the world of day trading. The trader tries to make small profits within a few seconds of beginning trade. Scalpers try to go for the top few stocks from each category in order to profit from trade. They will constantly have their eye on the stocks and quickly make a move as soon as the price reaches their desired point.

Scalpers can be the same as high-frequency traders and make money by engaging in many trades at once. The profit per trade might not look like much but the collective profit can end up being quite a big sum, but scalping is not for everyone, as it needs quite a bit of experience and quick decision-making. This can only be possible if a trader has been in the industry for a reasonable period. The prices can move within microseconds and, thus, it will be important to make faster decisions. Some of these decisions should be taken in microseconds. Thus, if a computer is made to take these decisions then it will be quite easy to carry out the trades. The computer can make the decisions in no time and make it easier for the trader to carry out the trade.

The shorter time frames are ideal as they can limit the exposure to risk and the scalpers do not have to worry about the price falling owing to large swings. They will be engaged in a trade only for a few seconds.

It is also easier to get smaller profits compared to bigger ones. The market will move slowly and thus it will be easier to capitalize on smaller movements. Thus, these markets are ideal for scalpers. If there are consistent smaller movements then they are easier for scalpers to adopt. They can use automated trading to find the right entry and exit points.

Scalping, however, has been questioned by some sections of traders who call it a lower form of trading, but as long as a strategy is making a trader some money, it can be considered to be a good strategy. After all, traders take part in trading to make profits and will not be too bothered by the method they adopt. The trader does not have to be extremely smart or qualified and just a little action in the right direction can help them make profits. That is exactly what scalpers try to do.

The last type of automated trading that people

take up is known as transaction cost reduction. Algorithms are used to break down large orders into smaller ones and then they are entered into the market in order to get the best price available.

Some markets can move the large orders and institutional investors will use automated systems to break down their orders into smaller bits. These can be absorbed more easily into the market without modifying the prices too much.

Thus, algorithms can be quite important for this type of trading. Again, computers will do a much better job at this compared to humans.

## Why Should You Use a Trading Algorithm?

As you have already seen, there can be many advantages and disadvantages associated with algorithm trading. You can go through them again to decide whether you want to use it or not.

Computers can be much faster compared to humans. The time taken to process can be cut down to the bare minimum which means trades can be automatically executed with ease. They can also be more accurate.

Computers can make decisions and act faster than human traders. There doesn't need to be constant monitoring. Traders do not be actively involved in the decision-making process.

Automated trading systems can be cheap to use and scale down the operations. It is better to make use of automated services compared to hiring a broker, as he might not be able to execute trades as fast or efficiently. If you wish to become a day trader, then it will be advisable to use a bot or automated trading that is specific to day trading.

If you plan to use automated trading then it is advisable to venture into Forex, Futures, etc. This will expose you to the different market conditions and tell you where the technology is best implemented.

You might need a little help regarding the type of

automated trading that you must adopt. Understanding the rules can help you trade with ease. You can also code the programs and make strategies that suit your particular needs. You must codify it based on what you are going for and what you want the trading system to do for you. You will be able to shift your focus to other things and do not have to keep your eyes glued to the monitor to keep up with any changes that happen in the stock's prices.

But bear in mind the negatives associated with automated trading and how they can impact your trades. Automated services might not always work for you. They can end up making losing trades as well. If the system ends up entering into a losing trade and you are unable to get out fast, then it can lead to losses. In fact, it might start moving you away from your gains and push you into loss territory.

One good way to prevent this is by engaging in risk management practices. Trading systems will do what you ask them to do and if there is a scenario that you have not considered and put checks in place then the system can end up going into a losing trade and you might end up losing money.

Using risk management can help you in such a scenario. You can set up a stop loss limit on each of the trades so that even if the system automatically ends up going through with a losing trade, the stop loss can prevent a loss from taking place. It would be ideal to set up a stop loss limit of 5%. You will also have the choice of shutting the system down in case the trade is not moving according to plan. All these steps can help you stave off a losing trade.

Some automated trading systems might not be flexible in nature. The computer will do exactly as you say. This might be a good choice for those who have to more control over their computer and trading. If a situation arises and the computer is not programmed to take it on, then it will automatically shut down. This can be a good thing as it will be easier to control the losses.

In this case, you will have to update and upgrade the system to make sure it is up to date. If the system ends up crashing, then you might have to reprogram it. It is best to be prepared in such a case so that you do not lose out on a winning position.

There was a crash that happened in 2010 when a majority of stocks ended up losing value. This was known as a flash crash and resulted in a loss of millions. This was a result of automated trading-high-frequency trading. It was found that many large trading firms had entered into a deal where large volumes were being traded. Most of them were being absorbed by high-frequency traders.

Just as they were absorbed by the traders, they were being sold off in a matter of seconds. This led to a hot potato volume effect as the same positions were being repeated. The stock volume kept fluctuating. As this was going on in the futures market, it ended up impacting the equities market owing to the arbitrage that was being tapped into. The companies were trying to take advantage of the differences in prices that existed between the S&P 500 stocks and the E-mini S&P contracts. Stock prices started going haywire and company stock prices began to rise high up. Some of them including P&G and Accenture began to trade at $100,000. This led to a very unlikely scenario in the market.

This led to a freezing of five seconds when the CME or Chicago Mercantile Exchange stop logic functionality was triggered off in order to keep a cascade of price decline from taking place. Within a short period of time, selling pressure within the E-mini rose up and there was an increased interest in the buying and selling of the stocks. Once the trading was resumed, the stocks began to recover, and the prices began to normalize.

As mentioned earlier, computers can come up with their own decisions and act on them faster than human beings. They can play a big role in generating market conditions such as the aforementioned scenario and end up leading to situations that are out of control. Nobody was prepared for such a situation, not even the trading exchanges.

Thus, it is not important to know or try to predict the future. Even if you think something is going to happen, something completely different might end up happening. It will be best to remain prepared for general situations that might occur. The market is bound to move up quickly and can also fall down just as quickly. It can help to be prepared for both these situations.

If you wish to come up with algorithms that are meant to make it easier for making predictions, then you must use platforms that are ideal for the same. Trading technology has evolved in a big way and it is no longer the same. There is no need to be an expert in the field in order to start programming. Someone with basic knowledge and skills can come up with the trading algorithms.

If you happen to have a trading system, be it one that is based on indicator signals or pure price action indicators or something based on technical analysis, you will be able to come up with a short script in order to keep an eye on the indicators of choice and then use them to your advantage. If you do not have the necessary programming skills, then you don't need to worry about it. You can always get someone to program for you. It can be a good idea to hire a freelancer who will be able to program it for you.

There are many trading platforms to choose from and each one has its own set of pros and cons. They will allow you to write your own trading algorithms and can be integrated into the infrastructure. You don't need to connect the exchange APIs, calculate the profit and loss, or worry about order execution. Systems are easy to adopt and implement and do not have to be modified. You can focus on the high value aspect of the trading operations. This can be the algorithm itself.

Some of the good trading platforms that are available are Catalyst and Quantopian. Quantopian is a good system to take up and is one of the more advanced systems of the lot. Catalyst is also a good system to adopt. They are both written in Python.

Some of them might offer paid services; it means that you can access better services by paying for them. The services might help you reach pivot points faster and more efficiently. The features can also help to monitor certain stocks that are interesting you. If there are any developments in their prices, then the system will alert you on the same.

If you are interested in back testing, then there can be many online portals that give you the chance to do so. You can test your algorithm over a certain period of time based on the past. This is a good idea if you wish to develop an algorithm and tailor make it to suit your needs. You can look up data from the past and work on predicting the future of the stock. You do not need to take risks and only invest in platforms that you are sure will work out well.

You can use your skill and expertise to come up with programs that can help you have a clear understanding of what the future can hold. Using automated trading is always a better choice compared to other types of trading, as you can be ahead of the game, but do not over rely on it and try to engage in some manual trading from time to time so that you can keep yourself updated with the market trends.

But do not over analyze things or engage in too much back testing as it might end up overfitting the strategy based on historical data. Your algorithm might work well for a specific price action during a particular point in time but might not always do well or go to plan for a chosen time frame. This is because market conditions are constantly changing, and it might take some time for your trading system to get adjusted to it. Thus, you cannot rely on back testing alone to gain the desired results.

If you do things the right way, then you can test your algorithm against unlimited scenarios in the future that might possibly arise. You don't need to understand all the aspects that will be involved or go into the testing. As long as you are able to work with the basics, you can come up with future predictions of the prices. It will be quite easy to generate the prices using the data at hand. It is not necessary to be too technical with it. Back testing can be enough.

Once you manage to come up with the strategy that is being tested, you must test it with a paper trader and live data to make sure there will be no problems in switching between back testing and live trading systems. You must make sure there are no programming errors as it can cause you to lose out on moneymaking opportunities.

If you think your strategy is working well when tested with the live data, then you can go ahead and open a trading account and deposit money and start trading using a bot.

These are some of the different aspects associated with automated trading that you must know if you wish to get started with it. Automated trading can be a great tool for both beginners and old hands. All you need is a simple trading toolkit that can be used to serve the purpose. Once you have it, you can convert your strategies into codes that the computer can use. This cannot be humanly possible, as you will need a computer's brain to do it. Thus, the best idea would be to use a computer and come up with the algorithms to trade instead of you.

But do not forget about the risks involved and how automated trading will never help you make 100% profits. Many factors can affect it including how it has been programmed, market conditions, etc. If you end up making a bad move, then you might have to compromise a winning position and move towards a losing one.

A good way to deal with it would be by setting a max drawdown limit that will kill the bot if it is triggered off.

It will be essential to make use of stop losses on all your trades. You will have to pay attention to all the small things that will be involved to make sure that you have a functional algorithm that can be used to develop a system that is near accurate. This doesn't just help you make more money but also helps cut down on the time required to make money. The saved time can be used to review the performance of the trading bot and work on improving the programs by building more bots in order to make more profits.

# Chapter 14 : The Difference Between Investing and Trading for All Traders

Remember that investing and trading are not the same thing and can be radically different things. They are two different methods of trading and trying to earn a profit from the market. The main goal of investing is to slowly build up wealth over a longer period of time by buying good stocks that will increase in value and holding on to them over a period of time. Apart from stocks, investors can also buy bonds and mutual funds as they too can be used to increase the value of the portfolio. Investors usually increase their profits by using compounding techniques or by simply reinvesting the profits and dividends that they have earned into additional stocks, bonds, etc. Most investments are held for longer periods of time that can range from years to decades in order for the intrinsic value to go up. This type of trader will not keep up with the day-to-day fluctuations that might arise and will only be concerned about the long-term benefits that can be amassed. There will always be a few inevitable fluctuations in the market and the traders will wait for it to ride out and wait for the rebounds. This type of trader or investors will be more concerned about the fundamentals of the stock including the price to earnings ratios and also manage the forecasting.

Trading is unlike investing and involves frequent buying and selling of stocks, bonds, futures, currencies, etc. The main goal will be to generate profits by investing in stocks that will change price faster and move up and down within a short time frame. Investors try to earn about 10 to 15% investment per year while traders will look for 10% return on a monthly basis.

Profits from trade are usually generated by buying the stocks at lower prices and holding on to them until the prices increase and disposing of them within a short period of time. Another tactic that is implemented is known as selling short where profits are made by selling at higher prices and buying at lower prices in order to take advantage of falling markets. Most buy and hold investors wait it out in order to come out of less profitable positions, traders must come up with profits or take losses for a specific period of time and use stop losses in order to close out positions that are not working out or are not generating enough profits even at the desired price levels. These traders will be more concerned about the technical aspects of the trade. These can include moving averages, stochastic oscillators in order to find profitable trading scenarios.

A trader's style of trading often refers to a timeframe or a holding period where the stocks or commodities or other trading instruments are bought and sold. These traders usually belong to one of the four following categories.

- Position Trader – here, positions are held for months to years

- Swing Trader – here, positions are held for

days to weeks

- Day Trader – here, positions are held throughout the day, but they will be disposed of by day's end

- Scalp Trader – here, positions are held for seconds to minutes without overnight positions

Traders usually choose their trading styles based on different factors that can include account size, the time that can be spent trading, the experience level, the risk appetite, etc. Investors and traders should both try to make profits based on market participation. Usually, investors try to get bigger returns over extended periods of time by buying and holding stocks. Traders, on the other hand, will try to take advantage of the rise and fall of the markets and take short positions and make several quick profits.

When it comes to making profits in the equity markets, investing and trading are the two main techniques that are adopted. They both come with different approaches and each one has its own set of pros and cons. It will be important to assess the pros and cons before deciding on any one of the techniques to adopt.

Here is a look at the main differences between the two.

## Holding Time

Trading is a technique where stocks are held for shorter periods of time. It can be for a week or just a single day. The trader is interested in the short-term profits. Investors, on the other hand, are more concerned about a stock's long-term benefits. They might hold on to it for a longer period of time that can be more than a year and is usually several years. A scalper is a trader who tries to dispose of the stocks within seconds of buying it. Scalpers try to capitalize on the smallest of movements in the market and can engage in several trades per day.

## Capital Growth

Traders look at the movement in the price of the stocks that are in the market. If the price goes up, then the trader will dispose it off. Trading requires skill and timing the market in order to generate wealth. Investors try to take advantage of compounding wealth and dividends over years and holding on to quality stocks.

## Risk Appetite

Both trading and investing involve risking capital. Investing can be a little less risky as the stocks will be held for longer periods of time and there will be no such pressure to dispose it off, but the returns might not be great unless the stock turns out to be a winner. There can be more risk involved with short-term trades, but the rewards can be much higher.

## Art vs. Skill

Trading is more like a one-day event that traders take part in and investing is carried out over an extended period of time. A day trader requires more skills and an investor needs to be patient. It is all based upon the overall sentiment in the market and the psychology involved. Investing can include understanding the basics of business and the commitments needed to remain invested for longer periods of time.

Traders who put their money into short-terms stocks buy and sell it fast in order to gain higher profits in the market. If they end up losing out on the right times, then they can incur losses. They try to look at the profit potential that might exist in the markets and book profits in the short-term instead of waiting for price action in the long-term.

It is entirely up to you to decide whether you want to be an investor or a trader. Both have their own pros and cons. It will be best to weigh each one up before deciding. You can also opt to be both.

# Chapter 15 : Simple Strategies to Make Money and Profits

Investing in the stock market is a great way to make money, be it active or passive. Using the right skills and approaches, you can easily make a lot of money, but it is not as easy as it sounds and requires dedication and hard work. Only then will you be able to make sizeable profits. This will not be an overnight task and will need a little time and effort from your end.

If you wish to make it big in the world of stocks, then here is a simple guide to follow.

## Putting Focus on Hot Stocks

Once you get started with the market, it will be important to focus on hot stocks. These refer to stocks that are doing well. For this, you must do your due research and identify patterns that exist and focus on the stocks that are doing well consistently. Stick with the same and grow with them. Avoid stocks that are hitting lows.

## Short Sell

Short selling is a concept that can help you make money regardless of the type of market you are investing in. Be it a bull market or a bear market, you can make money by short selling stocks.

## Cut Down Losses

Successful traders try to cut down their losses as fast as they can. This can help them make the most of their stock investments. It is not a good idea to dwell upon failures and focus on the future. If you have had an unsuccessful trade, then put it behind you and move on.

## Booking Profits

If you wish to be a successful trader, then you must book profits at the right time and do not hesitate to do so. If you wish to become rich through stock investments, then you must capitalize on the opportunities and not wait for something bigger or better to come your way. Embrace what you have if you want to succeed.

## Keep up

It will be important to keep up with the times and adopt new technologies. If you get left behind then you might not be able to make the same level of profits as the others. Do not be afraid to adopt technology and implement it. Right from using automated services to bots to monitor the market, implementing technology can help you make the most of your stock market investments.

## Liquid Stocks

It is important to pick stocks that are fast moving. Liquidity refers to how fast a stock moves or how liquid it is. The more the liquidity, the more chances you will be able to dispose of it faster; so, find a good stock and identify its up trends and capitalize upon it to make the most of your investments.

# Hype

Often, if you hear hype about a specific stock then it is best to stay away from it. Do not listen to hearsay when investing. Do your own research and confirm it before settling for a stock.

## Diversification and Leverage

Do not indulge in too much diversification and leveraging as it might not be the best way to go. It is best to stick with a few stocks that are promising and can help you make the most of your investments. Focus on a stock that is bound to do well and do not use any more than 30% of your investment allocation per stock.

## Basic Strategy

Your basic strategy can be customized to your liking and it does not always need to be about buying bottom and selling top. This does not always happen in the stock market. You must come up with strategy that will work for you.

There is no point looking for the top or the bottom. If a stock is doing well and has a good grip over the market, then consider investing in it.

## Make Plans

If you are looking for long-term profits in the stock market, then you must act accordingly to a set plan. Come up with a risk to reward specific plan that is tailored to suit your needs. Before getting started with it, you must stick with your curated plan and not stray from it.

But remember that the plan must be realistic. It might seem a little overwhelming to make profits in the stock market where everything is so competitive but a little effort in the right direction can help you achieve your targets. There can be a few minor setbacks and obstacles in the way but tackling them one by one can help you come closer to your dream and make the most of your money's worth.

# Chapter 16 : Long Term Strategies

The stock market can be quite uncertain, and it is never possible to predict the way in which a particular stock might move. It will be best to be prepared for any scenario that might crop up. Sticking to a few basic principles can help you stay ahead in the game and make the most of your investments. If you are looking for long-term success, then here are some rules to follow.

## Ride a Winner

It is essential to have a few winners in your portfolio if you wish to maintain consistent profits. Many who have experienced success in the stock markets attribute it to the presence of a few multi-baggers, but they hold on to these even after the stocks see quite a bit of rise in value. There can always be a little more upside to it and patience can pay off.

## Selling off Losers

It is important to get rid of stocks that are going nowhere as they can end up dragging you down. If there are any poor performers in your portfolio then cut them out before they end up damaging your portfolio. There is no shame in finding failures and fixing them.

## Hot Tips

If you hear news about a particular stock about to boom, then make sure you do your research on it first. There is no point chasing a hot tip without verifying it. Sometimes hot tips might work out but not always. Make sure you do your due research before investing based on tips.

## Small Stuff

Instead of worrying over a short-term investment that did not work out, it will be best to look at the long-term prospects. Remain invested and be confident in your investment. Short-term volatility will go away and make way for long-term success.

## Short Gains

Do not pay too much attention to the few cents that you might be able to make by disposing the stocks immediately. The long-term gains can be much more rewarding if you hold on to the investment.

## Price per Earnings Ratio

It is not important to fuss over the price per earnings ratio. You must not have too many metrics to stick to as it can end up confusing you and you might not be able to carry out proper analysis. A low price per earnings ratio might not always indicate that the stock is undervalued and a high price per earnings ratio might not always mean a company is overvalued.

## Penny Stocks

Penny stocks can seem like a good investment

vehicle, as they are cheap and can rise up quickly, but it is advisable to stay away from them if you plan on investing in stocks and not merely trading in them. Be it a $5 stock or a $2 stock, they might seem great at the beginning as you can buy a bunch of them but remember that not all are going to pay off the same way. It can be a risky move to hold on to penny stocks for the long-term.

## Future Oriented

It is important to be future oriented when dealing with long-term stocks. It does not matter if a particular stock is not doing well in the short-term. If it has potential to do well in the future, then you can invest in it. Some might be slow starters but once they start picking up the pace, they can end up growing in value much faster. It is best to focus on future potential and not delve into the past performance.

## Have an Open Mind

When you invest in the stock market it is important to work with an open mind. A company might not have a big name or might not be a household name, but it might be a good, debt-free company whose stock has a lot of potential. Investing in such a company can help you make more money. It will thus be quite important to go through the fundamentals of the company to make sure that it is a good one and has a lot of future potential.

## Tax

It is important to have tax in the picture but do not lay too much emphasis on it. Tax implications are an important topic to address but putting too much focus on it can lead to lower returns. The aim should be to minimize your tax liability and enhance your returns.

# Chapter 17 : Strategies for Options Traders

If you wish to make it big in the world of options trading, then here are some tips and tricks to bear in mind.

## Proper Capitalization

A common mistake that beginner traders tend to make is that they do not properly capitalize upon the leveraging options and offers. They are capable of turning a small amount into a fortune in no time if they make the right moves. Losing trades can be turned around into winning ones with just a few steps in the right direction.

## Risk for Appetite

Options traders have lower appetite for risk. Good options traders not only trade when there is lower appetite for risk and higher rewards at stake but also wish to have the odds in their favor. Most options traders will not try to make it big with every trade that they go through.

# Opportunities

One essential quality amongst options traders is that they have a lot of patience. Successful options traders do well when the odds are in their favor. They remain focused on the big picture and are not limited to things in the short-term. Some options traders simply observe the market and do not act until it is the right time. Beginner options traders are advised to do the same. It is better to wait on the sidelines and watch the market rather than jump in and take part in it.

## Market Cycles

Understanding and observing the market cycles is an important task. The idea is to understand what trades to undertake. An uptrend should be confirmed before acting. If a correction is taking place, then it is better to wait it out. Buying stocks in a confirmed uptrend is always a good choice and a conventional method to pick winning stocks.

## Trading Plans

Before options traders start trading, they come up with and implement a trading plan that will suit their requirements. The plan should be expressly written down so that it can be followed. Making a note of successes and failures can also ensure that you can revert to the plans. Trading should always be calculated and not random.

## Risk Management

Most options traders work with a solid risk management plan that helps to safeguard their investments. It will be important to work with one to ensure that risk is spread out evenly in the market. It is not wise to have a lot of money tied up in a single account. It should be spread evenly to ensure that the risk is spread out. As mentioned earlier, it would be best to limit the capital investment per stock to just 30%. If you have more than that invested in one place, then it might lead to risky trades. You must also set a fixed percentage of your capital as risk per trade. A good way is to set 5% as the minimum capital that you will be willing to risk per trade but if you are just starting out then this number can be lower. Once the trade has been placed, you must keep an eye on the risk levels and must not hesitate to keep up with your strategies. A good risk management plan can always help you make great trades and earn a lot of money but only if you take it seriously.

## Emotions

It is important to control your emotions when dealing in options trading. Good traders will control their emotions no matter the situation. Even if big losses come their way then they will not lose their cool and continue to engage in trade. Best traders keep their egos out of the mix and remain grounded. They do not get too attached to any particular stock and follow-predefined rules. A proper stop-loss in place can always help to ensure that emotions are kept in check.

## Disciplined

Options traders can be quite disciplined and will follow a strict trading plan. Even if it is quite difficult to wait out an opportunity, they will do so and only engage in trade when the right opportunity or situation comes along. They will never trade out of boredom or excitement, as it can be one of the worst things to do. Money management and risk management are both important no doubt but maintaining strict discipline is also essential for traders. Thus, if you wish to be a successful trader then you will have to maintain discipline and carry out the trade efficiently.

## Focus

Beginner options traders should not get carried away and remain focused on the task at hand. It will be essential to maintain a level head on shoulders to ensure that the right actions are being implemented. Just by staying focused on the task, options traders can make it big in the market. Going after goals and following rules and strategies will help. The strategies and rules you make should be customized to suit your liking and should not be pulled out of thin air or copied from someone else. This might not work out in your favor. A good trading plan can always get you out of a sticky situation and make sure you do not go back there again.

## Commitment

It is important for options traders to remain committed. If money is at risk, then it will be important to control the risk by taking the right measures. It will be important to keep an eye on the trading performances and stay up to date with the current news and events. If you are a beginner, then subscribe to a few newsletters so that you can remain abreast with the latest news.

## Back Testing

Back testing is an important aspect of options trading. All traders engage in back testing to evaluate the past performances. Past performances will not always repeat in the future but knowing how a certain stock or bond performed in the past can give the trader an idea of how it might function in the future. Not all back testing can be done manually as it takes a lot of time and skill. Thus, using back testing software can help traders assess the stock's past. Back testing can allow them to evaluate the pros and cons associated with the strategies they wish to implement. They can modify and adjust these to suit their needs.

## Time Period

The time period that is being used to back test is very important. If you end up testing a strategy between 1995 and 2000 then you might have some favorable results, but the same strategies might not have done well at a later time period. Thus, it will be a good idea to test out a strategy over a longer period.

## Sectors

It is important to consider the different sectors of the stock market. Focusing the strategy on just one sector will not be right. The sample taken to back test should be from different sectors. The sample size taken from the sectors should be large enough.

## Commissions

It is important to take commissions into account. If they are not accounted for then they can end up eroding the returns. You will have to adjust the expenses if your strategy involves constant trading.

## Past Performances

While some strategies worked out well in the past, they might not in the future. Thus, it will be a good idea to change the strategy every few months based on the situation at hand.

These are some of the tips to follow to become a
successful options trader.

# Conclusion

On that note, we have come to the end of this book. I thank you once again for choosing this book and trusting it as a guidebook for your options trading journey. I hope you found some good advice regarding day trading strategies and all your doubts and questions about day trading have been put to rest.

It will be essential to bear in mind that day trading can pay off only if you adopt the right strategies and remain patient. You might have to take risks along the way, as no form of trading can be risk free. You must make the effort of implementing the advice in this book so that you can make the most of your investments.

Remember that day trading is not rocket science and can be adopted by just about anyone interested in daily trading. It comes down to identifying the opportunities that come your way and making the most of them. You will have to increase your risk appetite so that you are able to trade freely.

Start small and then make bigger investments based on your risk appetite. Once you start getting comfortable, you can increase your investments accordingly.

You can consider going through the book again to understand the various day trading strategies that are involved and choose the ones that suit your trading style the best.

Thanks again.

# References

https://www.investopedia.com/articles/trading/06/daytradingretail.asp

https://www.investopedia.com/articles/trading/05/011705.asp

https://www.investopedia.com/articles/forex/11/why-trade-forex.asp

https://www.forexfraud.com/news/forex-trading-tips-20-things-need-know-successful-trader

https://www.investopedia.com/terms/s/swingtrading.asp

https://investinganswers.com/education/technical-analysis/swing-tradings-11-commandments-top-strategies-technical-analysis-2039

http://www.angelbroking.com/intraday-trading/tips-strategies

https://www.stocktrader.com/2007/09/12/60-

stock-tips-for-investment-success/

https://www.tradingacademy.com/resources/financial-education-center/10-day-trading-secrets-for-beginners.aspx

https://www.investopedia.com/university/beginners-guide-to-trading-futures/

https://www.investopedia.com/video/play/how-trade-futures-contracts/

https://www.investopedia.com/articles/optioninvestor/09/get-started-with-futures.asp

https://www.daytrading.com/

https://jbmarwood.com/day-trading-futures-living-tips-tricks/

https://upstox.com/learning-center/intraday-trading/intraday-trading-tips-and-tricks/

https://www.investopedia.com/articles/trading/11/automated-trading-systems.asp

https://medium.com/datadriveninvestor/how-automated-trading-can-increase-your-trading-profits-371ae1f828fe

https://www.investopedia.com/ask/answers/12/difference-investing-trading.asp

https://www.motilaloswalmf.com/knowledge-centre/5-keys-of-investing/5-key-differences-between-investing-and-trading/19

https://www.huffingtonpost.com/timothy-sykes/10-steps-to-becoming-a-st_b_8147928.html

https://www.investopedia.com/articles/00/082100.asp

https://www.moneyshow.com/articles/optionsidea-32534/